"With a passion for praying G[...]
lives and a deep desire to rais[...]
given the perfect resource fron[...]
encouraging stories, Scripture-b[...]
over seventy-five areas of a boy's life, *Powerful Prayers for Your Son* is
a must-read-and-give-a-copy-to-friends kind of book!"

Renee Swope, bestselling author of *A Confident Heart*,
former cohost of Proverbs 31 Ministries' radio show,
and praying mom of three

"Every parent wants what is best for their son. They long to see him
reach his God-given potential. Rob and Joanna Teigen give parents a
great gift of prayers that can unleash that potential! *Powerful Prayers
for Your Son* will be kept on my nightstand, right next to my Bible—
and the prayers will be kept in my heart!"

Pam Farrel, coauthor of *A Couple's Journey with God*
and *The 10 Best Decisions a Woman Can Make*

"Every parent with a son needs this heartfelt book. As a mother of two
boys, I continually strive to entrust them to God's care, and *Powerful
Prayers for Your Son* helps me do just that. Don't miss out on the
encouragement this book can be to you! You're going to love it."

Leslie Parrott, *New York Times* bestselling coauthor
of *Saving Your Marriage Before It Starts*

"I absolutely love this book! As a woman who loves to pray, and as a
mom who has raised three sons, I so wish I'd had this book when my
sons were growing up. Rob and Joanna Teigen have crafted a book
of prayers, Scripture, and stories that speak right to the heart of your
son's life. No matter his age, he needs your prayers. And no matter his
life stage, you are called to pray. God invites you to partner with him
to shape your son's character and his life. *Powerful Prayers for Your
Son* will help you to pray biblically based, passionate prayers specific
to the circumstances of your son's life. If you need a resource that
helps you engage your faith and pray with precision, look no further.
I cannot recommend the Teigens' book highly enough."

Susie Larson, author, radio host, and national speaker

POWERFUL PRAYERS

for Your

SON

POWERFUL PRAYERS

for Your

son

Praying for Every Part of His Life

ROB AND JOANNA TEIGEN

Revell

a division of Baker Publishing Group
Grand Rapids, Michigan

© 2014 by Rob and Joanna Teigen

Published by Revell
a division of Baker Publishing Group
PO Box 6287, Grand Rapids, MI 49516-6287
www.revellbooks.com

Repackaged edition published 2019
ISBN 978-0-8007-3543-2

Previously published in 2014 under the title *A Mom's Prayers for Her Son*

Printed in the United States of America

The Library of Congress has cataloged the original edition as follows:
Teigen, Rob.
    A mom's prayers for her son : praying for every part of his life / Rob and Joanna
Teigen.
        pages cm
    Includes bibliographical references.
    ISBN 978-0-8007-2261-6 (pbk.)
        1. Mothers—Prayers and devotions. 2. Sons. 3. Mothers and sons—Religious
aspects—Christianity. I. Title.
    BV4529.18.T43 201
    242'.8431—dc2   2014020061

In keeping with biblical principles of creation stewardship, Baker Publishing Group advocates the responsible use of our natural resources. As a member of the Green Press Initiative, our company uses recycled paper when possible. The text paper of this book is composed in part of post-consumer waste.

19 20 21 22 23 24 25   7 6 5 4 3 2 1

To our sons,
Joshua and Mason.
You are loved.

CONTENTS

12

ContentsContents

55. When He Needs a Good Example 139
55. When He Needs a Good Example 139
56. When He Needs to Wait 140

A Prayer Story 142

57. When He Needs His Parent 145
58. When He Has a Problem 147
59. When He Feels Pressure to Achieve 148
60. When He's Choosing Who to Worship 150

His Idols 152

61. When He Needs to Stay Close to God 156
62. When He's Becoming Mature 157
63. When We Need Time Together 159

A Prayer Story 161

64. When He Needs to Find Rest 163
65. When He's Attacked by the Enemy 164
66. When He's Discovering His Spiritual Gifts 166
67. When He's Critical of Others 168
68. When He Feels Pressure to Fit In 170

His Relationship with God 171

69. When He's Discontent 175
70. When He Doubts His Own Worth 177
71. When I'm Losing Hope in My Son 179
72. When He Has a Negative Attitude 180
73. When He Needs Motivation 182

A Prayer Story 184

A WORD *from* JOANNA

THE WRITING OF THIS BOOK finds me in a strange season of life. On the one hand, my oldest son is in college and has in large part "left the nest." I see his character, his hopes for the future, and his love for the Lord, and it brings me great joy.

At the same time there is a little boy in my home whom I desperately want to call my own. He came to us as a foster baby and we're struggling through a long, stressful adoption process. As of this writing, I'm still unsure what the final outcome will be.

As I look at both of my boys, I see with absolute certainty that every good thing in their lives and their hearts has come from God. No matter how much I care for and love them, I can't make them who I want them to be. I can't keep them safe. I can't control their future or their choices. I can't be the perfect mother I tell myself they need. I look at them and at myself and realize that without God, we are lost.

As that truth has taken deeper root in my heart and mind, it has pushed me to pray like never before. For many of my parenting years, I took a "my work PLUS prayer will get it done" approach. And while I am devoted to all five of my children, I now see that in the end my efforts will fade away compared to what the Lord brings about in their lives.

There is freedom found in placing my children in God's hands. When I release them to him, I am set free from worry. When I trust him to work out his salvation in their lives, I don't have to be their conscience and their judge. When I meditate on his constant love and mercy toward them, I can let go of resentment and anger over their weaknesses. When I believe in a Holy Spirit who is a counselor and guide, I don't have to be an all-knowing fountain of wisdom for every situation. When I pray and let God be God to them, I am free to just be me.

And so I pray. I pray with tears, pleading like everything depends on it. I pray over and over for the same things, and then pray for them again. And God gathers up my prayers and says, *Little one, you can rest. I hear you. I love you. I love your child. I am here, and I will always be. Be still and wait because I am going to do more than you can imagine.* And I dry my tears and take a deep breath, and I have peace.

Joanna

A WORD *from* ROB

MY WIFE IS AMAZING! I know I don't tell her that enough, but I am amazed at all of the tasks she juggles in a day. I read our family calendar on the wall with all its doctor and dentist appointments, kids' choir rehearsals, foster parent meetings, drop-offs and pick-ups, and it makes me want to go take a nap. Of course, while I'm napping Joanna is usually cooking dinner. Out of all the things my wife does for our family, the greatest are her prayers for us every day. It's a tremendous way that she demonstrates love for her family.

As a dad, I think of myself as a provider and protector of my kids. But I, too, have come to realize that prayer is the most significant way I take care of them. Our oldest son will celebrate his twentieth birthday soon. I asked him recently what it meant to him to know that his parents have prayed for him over the years. He said it has helped him to see the importance of his relationship with God, especially now that he's grown. It showed him how much we cared for his needs, both physical and spiritual. He believes our prayers protected him from a lot of things that he wasn't spiritually mature enough to handle along the way. And our prayers taught him how important prayer was in his own life with God.

It is through our prayers that we release our sons to God and trust him to care for them. We know that God can take our boys' struggles and failures and bring good from them. He can take their accomplishments and strengths and make them even greater when he's in control. He is willing and able to respond to any concerns or issues with our sons. We have taken to heart the truth that we can "approach God's throne of grace with confidence, so that we may receive mercy and find grace to help us in our time of need" (Heb. 4:16).

Another element of our prayers is that they're faithful and persistent. We know that we trust in a God who hears us when we cry out to him. Jesus taught his disciples that "they should always pray and not give up," and "will not God bring about justice for his chosen ones, who cry out to him day and night? Will he keep putting them off? I tell you, he will see that they get justice, and quickly" (Luke 18:1, 7–8). Don't lose heart! Keep on lifting up your son's concerns and needs to our loving Father every day. He will hear and answer your prayers. It may not be in your timing or in exactly the way you have in mind, but it will be in a way that brings glory to God and the very best for your child.

It's my hope that this book will encourage you to pray and believe in the God who is in control of everything. I pray it will bring you hope when your son has lost his way and your heart is breaking. I pray it will lead you to praise God for his power and limitless love for you and your son. Whether you pray straight through the book or pick it up when a certain issue is on your heart, expect the Lord to meet you right where you are. "Do not be anxious about anything, but in every situation, by prayer and petition, with thanksgiving, present your requests to God. And the peace of God, which transcends all understanding, will guard your hearts and your minds in Christ Jesus" (Phil. 4:6–7). God bless you.

Rob

1

When He Needs God's Salvation

Jesus said to her, "I am the resurrection and the life. The one who believes in me will live, even though they die; and whoever lives by believing in me will never die. Do you believe this?"

John 11:25–26

For God so loved the world that he gave his one and only Son, that whoever believes in him shall not perish but have eternal life. For God did not send his Son into the world to condemn the world, but to save the world through him.

John 3:16–17

What do you think? If a man owns a hundred sheep, and one of them wanders away, will he not leave the ninety-nine on the hills and go to look for the one that wandered off? And if he finds it, truly I tell you, he is happier about that one sheep than about the ninety-nine that did not wander off. In the same way your Father in heaven is not willing that any of these little ones should perish.

Matthew 18:12–14

LORD,
Thank you for the gift of my son. He has been created by you, and his life has been planned before the beginning of time. Your love for him is greater than I can comprehend. I know it is your desire that

he come to a full knowledge of you. I praise you for all the ways you have revealed yourself to him in his young life.

I pray you would complete your work of salvation in my son. Open his eyes fully to the truth of Christ—his perfect life, his complete atonement for our sins on the cross, and his resurrection that gives us the hope of life forever with you. Give him reassurance when he's doubting your Word. Rescue him from any temptation that might lead him away from following you. Provide wise teachers to instruct him in your ways. Fill him with your Spirit so he may know your voice and power in his life.

Thank you for all of your promises for my son. Let him experience your faithfulness—that no matter how far he may wander, you will seek him and bring him home. Show that you can be everything to him as his savior, helper, counselor, father, and friend.

Encourage me as his parent when my trust in you is shaken. Let me see my son through your eyes, no matter what sins or spiritual confusion he may wrestle with in his life. Never let me give up hope that he is in your hands.

Let me delight in the knowledge of you so my son can see joy and peace in me. Use me as an example of obedience and faith. Make my words full of praise and prayers, declaring your goodness in every situation we find ourselves in. Use me to lead him closer to you each day.

Thank you for holding my son so closely. Claim him as your own. May he live in you forever. Amen.

2

When He Feels Inferior

For you formed my inward parts; you knitted me together in my mother's womb. I praise you, for I am fearfully and wonderfully made.

Wonderful are your works; my soul knows it very well. My frame was not hidden from you, when I was being made in secret, intricately woven in the depths of the earth. Your eyes saw my unformed substance; in your book were written, every one of them, the days that were formed for me, when as yet there was none of them.

Psalm 139:13–16 ESV

And I pray that you, being rooted and established in love, may have power, together with all the Lord's holy people, to grasp how wide and long and high and deep is the love of Christ, and to know this love that surpasses knowledge—that you may be filled to the measure of all the fullness of God.

Ephesians 3:17–19

LORD,
My son looks at everyone around him and feels he doesn't measure up. He doesn't feel strong, smart, or talented. He doesn't feel valued or appreciated. He doesn't believe he has much to offer or that anyone would miss him if he wasn't around.

My son has forgotten who you say he is. Your Word says he is made in your image, and that what you made is very good (Gen. 1:27, 31). He needs assurance that his life is not merely an accident, but lovingly planned and created by you in every detail. Give him the power to trust in your incredible love for him that is beyond our understanding.

Thank you for the qualities that make my son who he is. I cherish his personality, his smile, and his unique outlook on the world. I see abilities and talents taking shape in his life. He is a gift to our family and has the potential to make the world a better place.

Help my son to find his worth in your eyes instead of comparing himself to those around him. Let him believe you are working in him, molding him into the valuable person you've always planned for him to be.

Guard my son's mind from dwelling so much on his own defeat and insecurities that he forgets how awesome you are. Let him find peace and total satisfaction in you and you alone. Let him "taste and see" that you are good, and realize that you are the source of every wonderful gift in his life (Ps. 34:8; James 1:17).

Use me to build up my son. Show me how to encourage him when he's feeling down. Open my eyes to his strengths so I can affirm him. Give me wisdom for how to guide him in overcoming his weaknesses and insecurities.

Thank you for creating my son and allowing me to share in his life. You are everything he needs—let him find his strength and joy in you. Amen.

3

When He Covets *More*

What causes quarrels and what causes fights among you? Is it not this, that your passions are at war within you? You desire and do not have, so you murder. You covet and cannot obtain, so you fight and quarrel. You do not have, because you do not ask. You ask and do not receive, because you ask wrongly, to spend it on your passions.

James 4:1–3 ESV

Do not love the world or anything in the world. If anyone loves the world, love for the Father is not in them. For everything in the world—the lust of the flesh, the lust of the eyes, and the pride of life—comes not from the Father but from the world. The world and its desires pass away, but whoever does the will of God lives forever.

1 John 2:15–17

F ATHER GOD,
    You know the deep selfishness in our hearts that craves our own
way. We want to make our own rules, come in first place, receive praise
and attention, and gratify whatever desire we feel at the moment. We
believe the lie that a material possession or fun experience will bring
happiness and satisfy our hearts.

Protect my son from loving the blessings you've given more than
he loves you. Give him gratitude for all you've provided so everything
he has can be a symbol of your kindness and generosity. May he find
his greatest delight and satisfaction in his relationship with you and
the people you've placed in his life.

Help my son to understand that the money, fame, or exciting experiences he may obtain in this life will only pass away. Set him free
to pursue "a treasure in heaven that will never fail, where no thief
comes near and no moth destroys. For where your treasure is, there
your heart will be also" (Luke 12:33–34).

Open his eyes to see any areas where he's coveting the things of
the world. Fill him with a greater love for his siblings and friends so
he can be generous and take turns. Give him gratitude for what he
has instead of begging for more and more when we're shopping. Set
him free from a complaining spirit that always wants more fun, less
work, and preferential treatment.

Teach my son to go to you for everything he desires. Change his
heart through prayer to want what *you* want for him. May your Spirit
move powerfully in his heart to create gratitude, patience, and love
for others. Give him your joy that is greater than any happiness this
world could offer.

Thank you for loving my son and offering the hope of complete
fulfillment in you. Amen.

4

When He's Standing Up
for What's Right

"For the eyes of the Lord are on the righteous and his ears are attentive to their prayer, but the face of the Lord is against those who do evil." Who is going to harm you if you are eager to do good? But even if you should suffer for what is right, you are blessed. "Do not fear their threats; do not be frightened."

1 Peter 3:12–14

Speak up for those who cannot speak for themselves, for the rights of all who are destitute. Speak up and judge fairly; defend the rights of the poor and needy.

Proverbs 31:8–9

LORD,
My son is like every other boy—he's fascinated by heroes who use their powers to save the day. Whether it's in a movie, a video game, or a book, he admires the skill and strength that brings victory in battle.

Reveal to my son that he can be someone's hero too. Give him courage to stand up for those around him who are weak or struggling. Let him be an ally for kids who are suffering at the hands of bullies. Give him discernment to know the difference between tattling and reaching out for help for those who need it.

Fill my son with compassion for the poor. Make him eager to share what he has so he can relieve the suffering of others. Keep him from a "me first" attitude through a desire to give and serve. Give him humility to treat everyone with respect, no matter their appearance or social status.

Make my son a man of integrity. May he play fair, speak the truth, and insist on justice if he sees someone being cheated. Give him a bold voice to speak up, and use his example to encourage other young people to stand for what is right.

Let my son know you are with him. You are aware of every time he reaches out to those who are rejected, helps someone in need, and stands up for someone who needs support. Show him that you have blessings and rewards in store for him, especially when it's costing him to do the right thing.

Use me as an example to my son through my attitude toward the handicapped, the poor, and the marginalized. Give me opportunities to help and honor others. Show me how to encourage my son to be bold and stand for justice.

Thank you for being our great hero and rescuer. Thank you for your power to rescue us from our sins and the enemy of our souls. Help us to always depend on you, our "ever-present help in trouble" (Ps. 46:1). Give us your strength and heart of compassion that cares for all people. Amen.

5

When He's Afraid

The Lord is my light and my salvation—whom shall I fear? The Lord is the stronghold of my life—of whom shall I be afraid? . . . For in the day of trouble he will keep me safe in his dwelling; he will hide me in the shelter of his sacred tent and set me high upon a rock.

Psalm 27:1, 5

I sought the LORD, and he answered me; he delivered me from all my fears. . . . This poor man called, and the LORD heard him; he saved him out of all his troubles. . . . Taste and see that the LORD is good; blessed is the one who takes refuge in him.

Psalm 34:4, 6, 8

F ATHER,
A child has so much to be afraid of—strangers, the dark at night, getting lost, embarrassment or failure at school, rejection by friends, and the disapproval of his parents. Some boys even have to fear violence, poverty, and being alone in the world.

Please encourage my son with your power and strength. Assure him of your promises to protect and care for him. Give him unwavering faith to believe you hear his prayers and are waiting to relieve all his worries. May trusting in you give him courage to face every person and situation that comes his way.

As his parent, may I never be a source of fear in his life. Keep me from out-of-control anger that will destroy his trust in me. May I be a strong protector of his body, his mind, and his emotions. May my words and actions be gentle and kind by your Spirit. Give me wisdom to know when to set boundaries for his safety. Give me courage to say no to people or experiences that could place him in harm's way, even if he doesn't agree or understand.

Sometimes my son is fearful and resists new opportunities or challenges. Help him to step out and try new things even if it's uncomfortable at first. Keep fear from taking control of his decisions. Give us both the wisdom to know if his fears are based simply on emotions or real threats to his well-being.

Thank you that we never have to be afraid to come to you. You love us perfectly, and "perfect love drives out fear" (1 John 4:18). Teach my son that he can run to you with every sin, worry, doubt, and battle he will ever face—you welcome him into your mercy with open arms.

You are our stronghold and shelter. May we make you our refuge every day of our lives. Amen.

6

When He's Angry

Be angry and do not sin; do not let the sun go down on your anger. . . .
Let all bitterness and wrath and anger and clamor and slander be put
away from you, along with all malice.

Ephesians 4:26, 31 ESV

Better a patient person than a warrior, one with self-control than one
who takes a city.

Proverbs 16:32

My dear brothers and sisters, take note of this: Everyone should be
quick to listen, slow to speak and slow to become angry, because
human anger does not produce the righteousness that God desires.

James 1:19–20

But you, Lord, are a compassionate and gracious God, slow to anger,
abounding in love and faithfulness.

Psalm 86:15

FATHER,
Sometimes my son's anger can explode without warning. It
makes anyone within range want to duck and cover before they or
their feelings come to harm. At other times he quietly boils for days as
he holds on to resentment toward whatever "enemy" has frustrated his
desires. Either way, his anger alienates him from others and from you.

Soothe my son's spirit and teach him self-control. Give him humility so he is free from the frustration of pursuing his own way in
everything. Soften his heart toward others so he can forgive instead
of allowing bitterness to take hold.

When my son becomes frustrated and angry, help him to think before he speaks. Keep him from lashing out at others with his words or his fists. Give him patience to listen before he reacts and to pursue peace instead of revenge. Help him to understand that giving way to anger only inhibits maturity and the "righteousness that God desires" (James 1:20).

Show my son the amazing truth that strength and power are shown in patience and self-control. May he master his impulses that want to jump into a fight and win at any cost. Keep him from being ruled by his emotions—may he be governed by your Spirit and truth. Make my son a compassionate, gracious person that seeks the good of others. Purify his heart from selfishness and animosity toward anyone.

Use me as an example of kindness. May I demonstrate patience and understanding with my son in every circumstance. Keep our relationship free from anger toward one another, and may we end each day in peace.

Thank you for your limitless love and patience. Thank you that no matter how many times my son may lose his temper, you will bear with him and help him to overcome his weakness. I pray you will receive all the glory as my son and I grow in becoming more like you. Amen.

7

When His Life Is Set Apart

What agreement is there between the temple of God and idols? For we are the temple of the living God. As God has said: "I will live with them and walk among them, and I will be their God, and they will be my people."

Therefore, "Come out from them and be separate, says the Lord. Touch no unclean thing, and I will receive you."

And, "I will be a Father to you, and you will be my sons and daughters, says the Lord Almighty."

2 Corinthians 6:17–18

But you are a chosen people, a royal priesthood, a holy nation, God's special possession, that you may declare the praises of him who called you out of darkness into his wonderful light. Once you were not a people, but now you are the people of God; once you had not received mercy, but now you have received mercy. Dear friends, I urge you, as foreigners and exiles, to abstain from sinful desires, which wage war against your soul. Live such good lives among the pagans that, though they accuse you of doing wrong, they may see your good deeds and glorify God on the day he visits us.

1 Peter 2:9–12

A LMIGHTY GOD, Thank you for your great mercy that enables my son to become your child. You have the power to bring him out of the darkness of this world into your wonderful light. He is offered the gift of an eternal home among your people. You can set him free from the power of sin. You promise to give him your constant presence in his life and his heart.

These are incredible truths, but they can fade from his mind when the tangible world seems more real than his spiritual identity. He can forget who he really is in you when he's overwhelmed by the temptations and pressures of this life.

Help my son to remember that he's been set apart. May he pattern his attitudes, words, and behavior after the perfect example of Christ. May he set his hope on the inheritance and rewards you have promised instead of striving for the attention and praise of others. Spare him from becoming so compelled to fit in with the world that he abandons his true identity as your child.

Keep my son from loving what the world loves. Guard him from the traps of money and popularity. When temptations come his way, give him strength by your Spirit to resist and do what's right. May his integrity, purity, and godliness bring glory to your name.

Give him endurance to live for you even when it's difficult. Build him up in those times that he's misunderstood. Labeled. Left out. Help him to trust you are with him even when he feels alone.

Give me wisdom to know how to encourage my son. May my devotion to you and your ways set an example of faithfulness. Let us have endurance to "throw off everything that hinders and the sin that so easily entangles. And let us run with perseverance the race marked out for us" (Heb. 12:1). Be glorified in our lives as we live fully for you. Amen.

A Prayer Story

When our son, Bo, was preschool age, tears flowed from his big blue eyes as I pulled into the carpool line. Not just the first day, but for days on end. Over time, he adjusted and enjoyed his class and teacher. But it ended there. Bo never wanted to go on playdates with the other kids. If they invited him to a birthday party, I had to stay there with him.

Then kindergarten came along. Same story. Tears fell as I walked him to his classroom each and every morning. Bo clung to me. One day, he even snuck out the side door of his school before school began. Over time, he again grew comfortable. But playdates had to be at our house, and no spend-the-nights at all.

Every new school year, every new Sunday school class, every new team brought this same response. My heart broke. What had I done wrong?

Bo and I read the Bible together every night before bed. One particular night, we read the story of Joshua. God's words to Joshua leaped off the page and into my heart: "Be strong and courageous. Do not be frightened, and do not be dismayed, for the LORD your God is with you wherever you go" (Josh. 1:9 ESV). I began to pray this verse over Bo. A few days later, I wrote him a letter sharing this verse and how God loved him as much as Joshua. How God wanted Bo to be strong and courageous, like Joshua. To step out and make new friends. To travel to new places.

Bo posted my letter on his wall. He memorized that verse. Over time, he spent a few nights out here and there. But still no retreats or youth group trips. Only one-nighters at houses within a block or two of ours. But I continued to pray boldly for God to give Bo the courage to say yes.

When Bo was fifteen, God opened the door for that yes through Young Life. It was an extended, out-of-state trip. At first he said no. His sister encouraged him to go, sharing that it had been the best trip of her life when she went. So he agreed. But the morning of the trip, he was nervous to go, hesitating as he stepped out of the car. But the moment he saw his friends, he took off. As I drove away, waving at my sweet boy through the window, tears leaked from my eyes as I praised God for answering the cry of this mother's heart. It took many years and a mountain of prayers, but God was faithful.

Tucked safely in Bo's bag was this Scripture-filled prayer.

Now at sixteen, thanks to God working through his Word and prayer, Bo is a strong and courageous young man.

....

Wendy Blight is a national speaker with Proverbs 31 Ministries and the author of *Hidden Joy in a Dark Corner* and *Living So That: Making Faith-Filled Choices in the Midst of a Messy Life*. Wendy, her husband, and their two children live in Charlotte, North Carolina.

8

When He's Looking for God

So I say to you: Ask and it will be given to you; seek and you will find; knock and the door will be opened to you. For everyone who asks receives; the one who seeks finds; and to the one who knocks, the door will be opened.

Luke 11:9–10

As the deer pants for streams of water, so my soul pants for you, my God. My soul thirsts for God, for the living God.

Psalm 42:1–2

Jesus answered, "Everyone who drinks this water will be thirsty again, but whoever drinks the water I give them will never thirst. Indeed, the water I give them will become in them a spring of water welling up to eternal life."

John 4:13–14

Lord,
       We come into this world with a thirst in our hearts that never feels satisfied. We look for "water" in financial prosperity, a successful career, praise and popularity, athletic achievement, and our physical appearance. Yet after we have filled our cup with all these things, our hearts remain as dry and lifeless as when we began.

Create a deep desire in my son for you and you alone. Teach him that he will only find true satisfaction in you. Help him to discover you, to know you personally, and to walk faithfully with you every day of his life. Keep him from trying to replace you with things that will only pass away and leave him disappointed.

Allow my son to experience your living water—your salvation through Jesus Christ. Show him your faithfulness through answered prayers, the encouragement of the Bible, and your good and perfect plans for his life. Let him discover that the answer to all of his longings lies in you alone.

Fill me with a deep yearning for you as well. Keep me from ignoring my thirst when I become distant from you for any length of time. Guard my mind from believing that any dreams, possessions, or achievements could replace the joy of living in your perfect will. Help me to focus on you instead of becoming distracted by the work, relationships, and media that clamor for my attention. May you always be my greatest love and the treasure of my heart.

Give my son an authentic relationship with you that is as real to him as anything he can see with his eyes. Make him so excited about knowing you that he's eager to share your living water with other seekers. Give him opportunities to tell how you've answered prayers and brought marvelous gifts into his life. May he continue to seek you every day of his life, with an insatiable desire to know you more and more. May we praise you together for your great love that allowed us to find you and be saved. Amen.

9

When He Must Submit to Authority

Let everyone be subject to the governing authorities, for there is no authority except that which God has established. The authorities that exist have been established by God. Consequently, whoever rebels against the authority is rebelling against what God has instituted, and those who do so will bring judgment on themselves. For rulers hold no terror for those who do right, but for those who do wrong.

Do you want to be free from fear of the one in authority? Then do what is right and you will be commended.

Romans 13:1–3

Have confidence in your leaders and submit to their authority, because they keep watch over you as those who must give an account. Do this so that their work will be a joy, not a burden, for that would be of no benefit to you.

Hebrews 13:17

L ORD,
  With each passing year my son becomes eager for more freedom and independence. He looks forward to earning his own income, driving a vehicle, pursuing adventure, and taking responsibility for his own decisions. There will never come a day, however, when he is without authority and boundaries in his life.

Thank you for our government that provides safety through laws and military protection. Help my son to treat law enforcement and elected leaders with respect. Give him self-control to obey the rules and regulations of our country and community. Guard his heart from rebellion that would deny the authorities you have put in place. May he submit with an attitude of surrender to you.

Help my son to see that submission brings freedom of its own. He'll avoid the painful consequences of a ruined reputation, lost income, damaged property, and personal injury. He'll be free to enjoy respect, liberty, and safety.

Guard my son from those who would influence him to break the law, for "bad company corrupts good character" (1 Cor. 15:33). Make him mindful of how he could end up in the wrong place at the wrong time, finding himself guilty by association with the crowd.

Begin shaping his heart attitudes today. Give him a respectful spirit toward his teachers and coaches. Let him practice obedience at home as preparation to submit to future leaders in his life. Bring rewards and commendation for his obedience, so he can see that living by your ways results in blessing.

Let my son's submission come from a commitment to living for you. May he love you with all of his heart and desire to please you in every way. May his life allow a clean conscience so he can walk before every authority with peace and confidence.

Bless those of us who watch over my son each day. Let us have joy in his obedience. Guide us by your Spirit to teach him well and protect him with diligence.

Thank you for your great love and care for my son. Amen.

10

When He's Going through a Storm

That day when evening came, he said to his disciples, "Let us go over to the other side." Leaving the crowd behind, they took him along, just as he was, in the boat. There were also other boats with him. A furious squall came up, and the waves broke over the boat, so that it was nearly swamped. Jesus was in the stern, sleeping on a cushion. The disciples woke him and said to him, "Teacher, don't you care if we drown?" He got up, rebuked the wind and said to the waves, "Quiet! Be still!" Then the wind died down and it was completely calm. He said to his disciples, "Why are you so afraid? Do you still have no faith?" They were terrified and asked each other, "Who is this? Even the wind and the waves obey him!"

Mark 4:35–41

ALMIGHTY GOD,
    You know the storm my son is experiencing. He has fears about his circumstances, that he'll be overwhelmed by more than he can handle. He feels alone in his struggle and sometimes wonders if his prayers make a difference. Sometimes he tries to just put on a

brave face, as if struggling means he's weak or a failure. He's not sure how to express how he's feeling, so he's acting out in difficult ways and making it hard to get close.

We can be like the disciples, believing God is sleeping and oblivious to what we're going through. Or a storm comes along and we put every effort into "bailing the boat" and solving the problem by ourselves. It isn't until our efforts are exhausted and hope is gone that we finally run to you for help.

Guide my son in how to find you in this struggle. Show him you are near and full of love for him. You are strong and kind—powerful enough to rescue him and loving enough to want to! May this particular hardship my son is going through become a story of your goodness in his life.

Give us strength to believe you use every difficulty for our ultimate good. You don't want us to just survive; you want to show your power and bring perfect peace. You promise to teach us perseverance, grow our faith, and display your glory through every hardship that comes our way. May my son find joy, knowing this temporary pain will deepen his knowledge of you.

Use me to help and encourage my son. Guard his heart from doubt. Strengthen his faith so he is more sure of you than anything in the world. Thank you for your power and love. Amen.

11

When He Needs to Tell the Truth

Better a little with righteousness than much gain with injustice.

Proverbs 16:8

No harm overtakes the righteous, but the wicked have their fill of trouble. The LORD detests lying lips, but he delights in people who are trustworthy.

Proverbs 12:21–22

Do not lie to each other, since you have taken off your old self with its practices and have put on the new self, which is being renewed in knowledge in the image of its Creator.

Colossians 3:9–10

LORD,
It is a challenge for my son to tell the truth in certain situations. I can see him fighting the temptation to lie in order to dodge responsibility, impress other people, avoid consequences, and even tear others down. He needs your help to guard his mind, words, and actions from giving in to dishonesty.

When my son would rather pursue his own fun than work hard at his chores or homework, give him integrity to give his best effort to the job at hand. Keep him from using deceit to cover up a lack of responsibility. If he fails to do what's required, give him humility to own up to it and strength to work wholeheartedly in the future.

My son feels pressure to stand out and be the best. Guard his words from embellishing his talents or accomplishments. Let him celebrate the achievements of others and encourage his siblings, classmates, and teammates. May he never present a false image in an attempt to draw praise to himself.

When my son makes the wrong decision or needs to correct his attitude, give him a humble heart that's willing to accept discipline. Keep him from hiding his mistakes and let him be quick to confess any wrongdoing. Give him courage to face the consequences of his behavior instead of denying or minimizing what he's done.

Sometimes a competitive spirit can take over my son's judgment. Keep him from pride that resents the abilities and blessings that others have. May he have kind, gracious words for others instead of lies or slander that hurt their feelings or reputation.

Use me as an example of honesty in my son's life. May I never compromise my integrity through gossip, little white lies, exaggerations, or false promises. Make me a keeper of my word, as you are always faithful and true to me.

Thank you for making us new and putting your truth in our minds and hearts. Amen.

12

When He Needs Wisdom

Blessed are those who find wisdom, those who gain understanding, for she is more profitable than silver and yields better returns than gold. She is more precious than rubies; nothing you desire can compare with her. Long life is in her right hand; in her left hand are riches and honor. Her ways are pleasant ways, and all her paths are peace. She is a tree of life to those who take hold of her; those who hold her fast will be blessed.

Proverbs 3:13–18

The fear of the LORD is the beginning of wisdom; all who follow his precepts have good understanding. To him belongs eternal praise.

Psalm 111:10

If any of you lacks wisdom, you should ask God, who gives generously to all without finding fault, and it will be given to you.

James 1:5

L ORD,
      Navigating our way through the choices and questions of life is
too confusing for my son to manage on his own. What classes should
he register for? What sport, musical instrument, or club member-
ship should he pursue? Which friends will be the best influence and
most fun to hang out with? Does the science lesson at school match
up with the Bible's creation story? What should his involvement at
church look like? Is it really worth saving sexual intimacy for marriage? There are so many options and messages coming his way—he
desperately needs your help.

Thank you for promising to give your wisdom whenever we ask.
You give us freedom to come to you with any question, knowing you
will "give generously without finding fault." Teach my son to look for
your truth and wisdom for his life. Give him ears to hear your voice
no matter how loudly the world may try to drown you out.

Bless my son with wisdom and understanding beyond his years.
Help him to find your path. Let him fear you in his heart and obey
you in everything. Fill him with your Spirit so he can discern right
from wrong and know your will for every decision he may face.

Use me as an example by the way I seek your wisdom for my life.
May I have a humble, obedient heart that looks for your perfect will
in every situation. Show me how I can best serve you in my home and
community, when to take on new challenges and when to say no, and
how to show the love of Christ to my son. Keep me faithful in prayer
and studying your Word, so I can discover your insight and truth.
Use me to encourage my son in seeking you when there's a decision
or challenge before him. Teach us both to wait on you when we ask
for wisdom, trusting you will respond instead of running ahead to
find our own way.

Thank you for your Word that gives perfect counsel. Give us your
thoughts and your truth so we know what to do and where you would
have us go. May we be fully yours and live in your ways. Amen.

A Prayer Story

M y son Joshua and I struggle with each other. He can be tender beyond belief, and I cling to those moments. But when he is upset, oh, it's best to walk carefully around him.

One of Joshua's "upset" moments occurred when he arrived home late for dinner. Again. Yes, he had called (when he was already late) and given his excuse. But this was one time too many. His reasons for being late never seemed to be "his fault," and although he clung to the same story this time, my husband and I decided he needed to be disciplined—or he was going to get into a very bad habit. So we grounded him for a few days. And he wasn't very happy with us. *Oh, well,* I thought. *Hope he learns to watch his time better!*

At bedtime the same night both Joshua and Matthew, my younger son, were in rare form. And I reprimanded them both several times. But Joshua kept pushing me, kept doing what he knew he should not do, kept moving closer to the edge, and finally he went over it. Got his computer time taken away for three days. (I started by taking away one day, but he kept going. So I did too.)

Then it was time to say good night. I visited my daughter, Elizabeth, and Matthew first—to give Joshua a little time to cool off. In retrospect, I think I would have needed to wait until the morning to have a rational conversation with him. But I didn't have retrospect at the time (think about that one for a minute!), so I went into his bedroom to say good night.

I listened to him ranting about how I had ruined his day, how it was unfair for me to ground him from leaving the yard and from using the computer, and how I was not doing a good job of raising him. He proceeded to tell me that my discipline was NOT going to teach him anything. He said he would NOT learn from it, and that it would NOT change his behavior. He said it would only serve to make him NOT like me more. And he reaffirmed that I was NOT a good mother.

I tried to tell him that I understood him not liking my decisions, but I hoped he would learn from them and that one day he would understand I was trying to do what is best—trying to raise him to be responsible and respectful because I love him and want good things for his life. He wasn't interested in listening and I realized I wasn't doing anything to help the situation, so I said good night and left his room.

As I walked out I prayed that God would help Joshua understand— I am for him, not against him. And that is when God led me to a new prayer. For quite some time I had been praying—in the middle of my struggles with Joshua—*Lord, show me his heart*. This prayer came at the suggestion of a speaker I heard once, as she was encouraging the audience to seek understanding in the midst of conflict. I do want to understand my son. I do want to see his heart. But this time, as I prayed that prayer, I added to it, *And, Lord, show him MY heart*.

It has been nearly five years since that incident with Joshua. He's sixteen years old now. And while we still have our conflicts, God has done something that absolutely delights me.

Every now and then our family gets into a discussion about how my husband and I have chosen to parent our children. There was a time when Joshua would bemoan the fact that his friends had it easier than he did, but very recently my son has admitted he understands we're making these decisions for his good. He doesn't seem to see me as the enemy anymore. (Not all the time, anyway!)

Honestly, I cannot attribute the change in Joshua to anything but a very faithful God. I have no idea how many times I have prayed that prayer over the years, but I trust God is, indeed, showing him my heart.

....

Karen Hossink is a popular speaker to moms' groups and the author of *Confessions of an Irritable Mother* and *Finding Joy: More Confessions of an Irritable Mother*. Learn more about Karen at www.irritablemother .com and www.surviving-motherhood.blogspot.com.

—— 13 ——

When He Needs Courage
to Live for God

Have I not commanded you? Be strong and courageous. Do not be afraid; do not be discouraged, for the LORD your God will be with you wherever you go.

Joshua 1:9

So we say with confidence, "The Lord is my helper; I will not be afraid. What can mere mortals do to me?"

Hebrews 13:6

Dear friends, do not be surprised at the fiery ordeal that has come on you to test you, as though something strange were happening to you. But rejoice inasmuch as you participate in the sufferings of Christ, so that you may be overjoyed when his glory is revealed. If you are insulted because of the name of Christ, you are blessed, for the Spirit of glory and of God rests on you.

1 Peter 4:12–14

LORD,
My son feels so much pressure to fit in with the boys around him. They treat foul language and crude humor like a badge of masculinity. Violent video games and R-rated movies can represent a false sense of maturity. They feel important and proud when they defy or disrespect adults and authority figures. It takes courage for my son to live by your ways, especially when he has to walk that path alone.

Give my son the strength to live for you without compromise. Equip him to stand firm in his faith, for "how can a young person stay on the path of purity? By living according to your word" (Ps. 119:9). Give him an assurance of your presence so that even if he feels left out and alone, he can know you are with him.

Reveal the amazing truth that he will receive a reward from you every time he's insulted for following you. Pour out your blessings in his life as a comfort and encouragement to keep on going. Guard his heart from fear—no insult or rejection compares to the glory you have in store for your children.

Show me how to encourage my son. Help me to celebrate with him every time I see your hand in his life. Give me wisdom to help him find friends and mentors who will stand with him in doing right. Let me walk beside him in our journey of faith so he doesn't have to make his way alone.

May we obey you because we love you more than anything. Guard us from living by the rules just to feel good about ourselves or to feel superior to others. Let us live by the Spirit's power, rather than our own weak efforts to do the right thing. Be our helper. Be our strength. Be our courage. And may we come nearer to the heart of Christ every time we pay a price for following you. Amen.

14

When He's Falling into Addiction

Don't you know that when you offer yourselves to someone as obedient slaves, you are slaves of the one you obey—whether you are slaves to sin, which leads to death, or to obedience, which leads to righteousness? But thanks be to God that, though you used to be slaves to sin, you have come to obey from your heart the pattern of teaching that has now claimed your allegiance. You have been set free from sin and have become slaves to righteousness.

                                                                    Romans 6:16–18

My eyes are ever on the LORD, for only he will release my feet from the snare.

                                                                    Psalm 25:15

L ORD,
      This world is a broken, painful place for my son to navigate as he grows. He'll experience physical illness and injuries. Trusted friends and family may betray his confidence. The dreams he holds for the future may crumble. Goals he works hard to achieve can end in failure. He may find himself lonely, broke, sick, or disappointed. As he looks for ways to relieve his pain or find distraction from his troubles, he may end up looking in all the wrong places.

Keep my son from the trap of addiction as he seeks comfort in this world. The pleasures of food, alcohol, sex, entertainment, drugs, and money can offer a temporary diversion from the pain in his heart. But these same pleasures can become a trap that steals his freedom to live in your peace and righteousness.

Don't let my son's heart become enslaved to anything or anyone but you. Let him find his greatest satisfaction in your presence. Give him discernment to identify temptations that come his way. May he have strength to "flee the evil desires of youth and pursue righteousness, faith, love and peace, along with those who call on the Lord out of a pure heart" (2 Tim. 2:22).

Surround my son with believers who will encourage him to walk in your ways. Give him humility to ask for help if he's overtaken by any sin. Open my eyes to see any areas of bondage that are developing in his life. Show me the boundaries to set to guard him from temptations that may be too hard to resist.

Show my son that you are his true comfort. You offer a future of perfect peace and love with you. Your plans for him are good and perfect. You are his one true, faithful friend. You are the source of everything he needs. You hold the answers to all of his questions. Let my son live in your freedom. Keep his eyes on you. May he offer his life fully to you and obey you with all his heart. Amen.

15

When He Needs to Stay Pure

Flee from sexual immorality. All other sins a person commits are outside the body, but whoever sins sexually, sins against their own body. Do you not know that your bodies are temples of the Holy Spirit, who is in you, whom you have received from God? You are not your own; you were bought at a price. Therefore honor God with your bodies.

1 Corinthians 6:18–20

For the grace of God has appeared that offers salvation to all people. It teaches us to say "No" to ungodliness and worldly passions, and to live self-controlled, upright and godly lives in this present age, while we wait for the blessed hope—the appearing of the glory of our great God and Savior, Jesus Christ, who gave himself for us to redeem us from all wickedness and to purify for himself a people that are his very own, eager to do what is good.

Titus 2:11–14

LORD,
It seems as if my son is under attack from countless forces that would steal his innocence. He is bombarded by images on magazine covers at the grocery store, the pornography that can flash on our computer screen despite parental controls, the larger-than-life photographs of lingerie models at the mall, and the "family" programming

on television that portrays sexual intimacy outside of marriage as good and normal. Boys at school use crude humor and comment about girls' bodies as if these precious daughters of yours are merely objects. It seems like an impossible dream that my son can overcome lust and hold on to his purity until his wedding day.

Thank you for your wonderful promises of grace for my son. By your power he can find freedom from the traps the world has set to bring him down. May your Spirit be alive in his heart, teaching and purifying him every single day. Make him eager for what is good and ready to run from any temptation to dishonor God with his body.

Give my son a clear picture of the joy you have in mind for his future. Even now, create a loving heart toward his wife. Prepare him to cherish and honor her for a lifetime. Give him a brotherly, protective attitude toward every girl in his life today. Make him a trustworthy person, so any young woman will feel respected and valuable in his eyes. Let him keep his way pure so he can have the joy of a clear conscience with you and in his marriage.

Help me to be wise in teaching and guiding him. Give me courage to speak openly with him about dating, sex, and matters of the heart. Show me the boundaries to set to protect him from temptations that are too much for him to handle. May I be pure in my heart and life, in how I speak, the entertainment I choose, and in my relationships so my example to my son is never compromised.

I know with you all things are possible, including the protection of my son's purity and innocence. Stay near to him and keep him close to you. Amen.

His Relationship with His Mom

Be completely humble and gentle; be patient, bearing with one another in love. Make every effort to keep the unity of the Spirit through the bond of peace.

Ephesians 4:2–3

He's wore a hole clear through the left knee of those pants, lanky life coming out everywhere. Soon enough, this boy's a man, I can see it. There is a way a mother can hold a son safe, a way that she can cup exactly who he is in an unconditionality, a love that cradles like a radical grace. Am I too old to learn?

Ann Voskamp[1]

Over the years of raising my children, I've found myself taking on many different roles in their lives. I've been caregiver and nurturer. Teacher and counselor. Chauffeur and social coordinator. Chef and personal shopper. Disciplinarian and provider. Playmate and friend. As my kids have grown and their needs have changed from year to year, my place in their life has adjusted as well. In times of transition, as they become more independent and capable, I've had to adapt to becoming less hands-on and letting them go.

I've also seen how my sons need different things from me compared to what they look for from my husband. He's much better at playing with trucks and running around the backyard with the boys, but if they're hurt, hungry, or want to know the day's plan, they come straight to me. I've come to realize that I don't have to be all things for them—they benefit from a variety of experiences with the ones who love them.

It seems that two things especially speak to my sons' hearts—physical care and praise. It's cliché to say that the way to a man's heart is his stomach, but my sons feel loved by me when the kitchen is stocked with bags of apples and Costco-sized jars of peanut butter. Add some chocolate milk and donuts to the mix and they *really* feel warm inside! For my oldest son, knowing his work uniform has been laundered, his shampoo has been replaced before it runs out, and the porch light will be on when he comes home late all convey that I care and that he's important to me.

Over the years I've also seen how much my words have an impact on my oldest son. It means a lot when he hears me tell my friends and extended family how proud I am of his hard work. When I correct his sisters for rudeness to their brother, or if I ask his opinion about a decision I'm facing, it says he's worthy of respect. He still wants to know if I like his haircut and he models his new sweaters for my approval. There's something unique about the honor and affirmation I give to my son—it affects his sense of worth in a powerful way.

For my younger guy, praise has a wonderful effect on his behavior. He likes to show me how hard he can kick a soccer ball and the pages he colors in Sunday school. When I cheer him on for cleaning up his toys and petting our rabbit with gentleness, he glows and is motivated to do a good job the next time too. As much as I can, I encourage him with high fives and applause. It brings a positive note to our days, which can otherwise feel taken over by time-outs and scolding.

The Bible says that wives are to respect their husbands (Eph. 5:33). Respectful words and behavior are significant to our sons as well, and teaches them what an honoring relationship looks like before they marry. I pray that God will give me a quiet and gentle spirit toward my husband and keep me free from a critical attitude, so my sons can have a lovely picture of God's design for relationships lived before them.

When I think back to the times when closeness to my sons has been the most tested, it almost always relates to how much grace and time they receive from me. When I'm quick-tempered and flare up over little mistakes, they run for cover! If I have unrealistic expectations that are beyond their experience or maturity level, they feel insecure and lose their motivation. When I put our to-do list ahead of time together, they don't feel important or valued. Patience, understanding, and unconditional love are what free my sons to share their hearts and lives with me.

My boys also like just knowing I am there. If I take the time to sit still beside them, they begin to talk and invite me into their hearts. My oldest will "dream a little dream with me" about love and college and travel. My little one cuddles up under my arm and lets me play with his dark, curly hair. We make eye contact. Thoughts and questions are shared. It takes so much effort for me to quiet myself and just listen when the sink full of dishes is calling and the laundry and emails never end. But my sons love to know that I will tune out the clamor and just *be* with them.

I love that I can talk to God about my relationship with my boys. He helps my heart to focus on their strengths rather than their weaknesses. I can ask for help to trust God to work out whatever battles they're fighting at the moment. He reminds me that nagging will never change their hearts—only the Holy Spirit can do it! When I want to hold on tight out of fear rather than setting them free to discover God's path to follow, he gives me peace to release them into his hands. He motivates me to be their greatest cheerleader, never giving up hope that God can do amazing things in and through them.

Mothering boys has been one of the most joyful adventures of my life. It's incredible to experience their energy, humor, and creativity. I pray that everything I do and say will express what a privilege I believe it is to be their mom. And I pray they'll know how deeply I love them, for they are my treasure.

16

When He's Proud

All of you, clothe yourselves with humility toward one another, because, "God opposes the proud but shows favor to the humble."

1 Peter 5:5

Do nothing out of selfish ambition or vain conceit. Rather, in humility value others above yourselves, not looking to your own interests but each of you to the interests of the others. In your relationships with one another, have the same mindset as Christ Jesus: Who, being in very nature God, did not consider equality with God something to be used to his own advantage; rather, he made himself nothing by taking the very nature of a servant, being made in human likeness. And being found in appearance as a man, he humbled himself by becoming obedient to death—even death on a cross! Therefore God exalted him to the highest place and gave him the name that is above every name, that at the name of Jesus every knee should bow, in heaven and on earth and under the earth, and every tongue acknowledge that Jesus Christ is Lord, to the glory of God the Father.

Philippians 2:3–11

FATHER,
When you created my son you blessed him with many talents and much potential. As he grows he's discovering new abilities and the unique characteristics that set him apart. You're equipping my son for excellence and opening doors for him to succeed.

However, my son has forgotten that you are the source of all his strength, and that any intelligence, skill, or reward comes from your hand. He's becoming proud. A sense of superiority is growing in his heart.

This pride is making him arrogant in his speech. He feels he deserves special attention or favor from others. He's giving himself credit for his accomplishments, rather than showing gratitude to you and those who have invested in his training. He's looking down on the achievements of others and coveting praise for himself.

This pride is creating a barrier in his relationship with you and with other people. He'll find himself outside of your grace if he persists in this opposition to you. Others will resent his attitude and he'll lose their friendship and respect. He'll end up alienating the ones who support him the most.

Soften my son and create a spirit of humility in his heart. Give him understanding to see you are his Creator and the source of every good thing in his life. Teach him gratitude for the skills you've given and the doors you've opened to pursue success. Let him sincerely applaud the achievements of those around him. May you receive the glory for every victory he celebrates.

Give me wisdom to know how to cheer him on while pointing him to you. Use me as a model of humility and servanthood to others. Let me be fully obedient to you—concerned with the troubles and interests of others and praising your name in every situation.

Dig up this seed of pride in my son's heart before it becomes deeply rooted in his character. Restore his ability to see your power and authority in his life. As he begins to see you as the giver of all good things, may he love you more and more. May he confess that Jesus Christ is Lord and commit his way to you. Amen.

17

When He's Grieving

The LORD is close to the brokenhearted and saves those who are crushed in spirit.

Psalm 34:18

Brothers and sisters, we do not want you to be uninformed about those who sleep in death, so that you do not grieve like the rest of mankind, who have no hope. For we believe that Jesus died and rose again, and so we believe that God will bring with Jesus those who have fallen asleep in him.

1 Thessalonians 4:13–14

Praise be to the God and Father of our Lord Jesus Christ, the Father of compassion and the God of all comfort, who comforts us in all our troubles, so that we can comfort those in any trouble with the comfort we ourselves receive from God. For just as we share abundantly in the sufferings of Christ, so also our comfort abounds through Christ.

2 Corinthians 1:3–5

FATHER,

My son has never encountered a painful loss like the one he is experiencing right now. He's hurting and confused. He's asking hard questions and wrestling with regret. He doesn't know how to move forward. He isn't sure how to express his emotions or if anyone understands. He's afraid that to feel this kind of sorrow is a sign of weakness.

You know exactly how he feels. You have suffered in ways we could never comprehend. This situation is part of your plan and you are in control. You are near and are full of compassion and comfort for each of us.

Use this experience to reveal your heart of love for my son. May he find you to be as close as you promise to be. May he sense your presence in a powerful way like never before. Give him faith to pray to you, and full assurance that he is heard.

Reassure my son that "weeping may stay for the night, but rejoicing comes in the morning" (Ps. 30:5). Give him hope in an eternal future with you where "God will wipe away every tear from their eyes" (Rev. 7:17). Help him to see that in you he will find his strength and joy once more.

Use this experience of grief to create compassion in him for those who are hurting. May he become tenderhearted and understanding, with a deeper sense of what Jesus's pain and sacrifice on the cross really means. Work in my son to make him like Christ—holding out hope and comfort to those in any kind of trouble.

Show me how to minister to my son right now. Give me words of encouragement to build him up by your Spirit. Use me as a source of love and help. Allow us to draw closer to each other as we carry this burden together.

Thank you for your great love, and your promise that "in all things God works for the good of those who love him, who have been called according to his purpose" (Rom. 8:28). You will use every heartache to reveal yourself to my son and bring him greater good than he could imagine. Amen.

18

When He Needs to Honor His Parents

Children, obey your parents in the Lord, for this is right. "Honor your father and mother"—which is the first commandment with a promise—"so that it may go well with you and that you may enjoy long life on the earth."

Ephesians 6:1–3

But mark this: There will be terrible times in the last days. People will be lovers of themselves, lovers of money, boastful, proud, abusive, disobedient to their parents, ungrateful, unholy, without love, unforgiving, slanderous, without self-control, brutal, not lovers of the good, treacherous, rash, conceited, lovers of pleasure rather than lovers of God—having a form of godliness but denying its power. Have nothing to do with such people.

2 Timothy 3:1–5

LORD,
       Out of your great wisdom and love you created *family*. In your Word you instruct us in how to relate to one another in our home. Part of your perfect plan is for children to honor and obey their parents.

You hold blessings in store for my son if he submits to my authority. You describe how his future will go well and how he'll enjoy a more fruitful life. You also describe the challenges my son will face in these days. We live in a time of rebellion and selfishness. Young people despise discipline. They disrespect adults. They celebrate their immaturity and lack of self-control. My son feels torn between what he knows is right—obedience—and the temptation to reject his parents and go his own way.

The push and pull between his will and mine is creating hard feelings between us. I'm weary of having to justify what I say and ask him to do. I feel on edge, expecting conflict to rise up at any moment. He ignores me or argues about nearly everything. I can sense his resistance to my input and his frustration with being asked to do things my way. We need your help to find unity and peace again.

Do a powerful work in my son's heart. Turn him toward you and help him to see his parents as a gift from you in his life. Let my words of correction and advice be received with humility. May he see my heart of love that seeks to guide and protect him rather than steal his freedom and joy. Build trust between us so he can have confidence in my motives and submit himself to my authority.

Give me wisdom to know how to pick my battles. Let my words be gentle and full of truth and love. Fill me with mercy and grace, just as you show patience with my own weaknesses. Keep my heart from resentment that expects the worst and is quick to find fault. May I walk in integrity so I'm worthy of respect. Open my eyes to my son's strengths and what is worthy of praise in his life. Show us the way to a right relationship with each other and with you.

Draw my son to you and give him the mind of Christ. Amen.

A Prayer Story

The morning of March 20, 2012, I was ready to start my day off with Jesus. The night before was a rough time with our teenage son, so I was looking forward to my devotion time. I sat down in my comfortable chair with steam rising up from my cup on the table next to me, and my Bible and devotional book in my blanket-covered lap.

What I thought was going to be my normal quiet time routine suddenly was taken in a different direction by God telling me to journal with a pen. I gave a quick argument that I do most of my journaling on the computer, not with ink, but he impressed it on my heart to get up out of my chair and go get a journal and pen. I remembered an unused journal I had received as a gift from a friend the year before and had stashed in a drawer, so I dug that out and returned to my chair ready to write.

Immediately I felt prompted to write out a psalm and personalize it about my son Aaron. *Easy enough*, I thought as I flipped through the book of Psalms. I read the first few verses of Psalm 119, and from what I knew that my son was going through, it seemed like a fitting psalm. I began to write verse by verse down in the pages of my journal, intertwining my son's name within each verse. As I wrote and my hand began to hurt, I looked ahead to see how many verses Psalm 119 had in it. At the time, I had no idea that Psalm 119 is not only the longest psalm but also the longest chapter in the Bible. "Very funny," I said to God, as I continued to write.

When I arrived to verse 126, I could not write it. I sat there and just cried. After many minutes, I finally wrote out, "It is time for you to act, Lord." I cannot explain to you why I was so bothered by that verse, other than as a Mom I knew I wanted God to get ahold of our son, but I wanted it done in a nice way.

Finally, after two hours of personalizing all 176 verses, cramps in my right hand, and two cups of cappuccino, I closed my journal and went about my day. Later that evening my husband came to visit me at work to tell me that two detectives had shown up at our house looking for our son. Over the weekend, he had been involved in a crime with three other men. I was sure they had the wrong kid, but the proof would shatter my hope that the detectives had made a mistake.

Later that night, as I was getting ready for bed, I remembered the journal. I woke my husband up and read each verse to him. We cried, held hands, and together we prayed over our son like never before. Hours after finding out our son was going to be charged with a felony, I realized why God had sat this mom down in her chair and interrupted her morning routine. I was always a mom who prayed that my son would have a "good day," and on this particular day only God knew that my son needed me to go deeper, ask more, be specific, and even shed tears. God needed me to storm the throne room with petition for him to act, and I had no idea as I sat in my chair and wrote in my journal that I was actually standing in the trenches for my teenager.

That day taught me how to pray for my son. It prepared me for May 23, 2013, as I sat in a courtroom with my family and listened to a judge sentence my son to prison. I cried that day and for the next three weeks nonstop, but I also prayed for him. I no longer pray my son has a "good day." Instead, I pray God interrupts his day, just as he did mine in 2012. I sat in my chair that morning ready to set out on my path of routine until God changed my route. Without my knowing, God transformed this mom with weak, hurried prayers into my son's very own personal prayer warrior as he led me onto the battlefield. The trenches are a much better place to be than in a chair of comfort and routine.

....

Lelia Chealey is a wife, mom, and joined the grandma club twice before she turned forty. She is a writer, speaker, Bible study leader, and the founder of the Refresh My Heart women's conference in Nebraska. You can connect with her at www.leliachealey.com.

19

When He's Stressed

Don't ever worry and say, "What are we going to eat?" or "What are we going to drink?" or "What are we going to wear?" Everyone is concerned about these things, and your heavenly Father certainly knows you need all of them. But first, be concerned about his kingdom and what has his approval. Then all these things will be provided for you.

So don't ever worry about tomorrow. After all, tomorrow will worry about itself. Each day has enough trouble of its own.

Matthew 6:31–34 GW

Do not be anxious about anything, but in every situation, by prayer and petition, with thanksgiving, present your requests to God. And the peace of God, which transcends all understanding, will guard your hearts and your minds in Christ Jesus.

Philippians 4:6–7

FATHER,
My son is stretched so thin. He feels pressure to succeed academically, live up to my expectations, please his friends, and achieve all of his ambitions. There aren't enough hours in the day to accomplish what is before him. He feels that no matter how hard he works, success is just out of reach. He worries he won't have what he needs today. He's tired. He's insecure. He's just not sure he has what it takes.

Give my son your rest. Help him to be still and know that you are God (Ps. 46:10). Let him release his hopes and plans to you, trusting you have him in your hands. May he rest in your promises to care for him and provide whatever is lacking for him today.

Teach my son to run to you in prayer with any worries on his heart. Give him gratitude for all the ways you've helped him in the past. Reveal that you are the source of all his talents and abilities—his success begins and ends in you.

Turn my son's heart toward you. Let him seek you first, rather than his own accomplishments. Let him seek your will instead of striving after his own hopes and dreams. May he live to give you glory rather than to make his own name great. And in this surrendering of himself, may he find peace and rest from the labor he is burdened with today.

Teach my son to trust you. You know his needs and what will happen tomorrow. Guard his heart from doubt and his mind from worry. Draw him to you in prayer. Fill him with peace that will guard his heart and mind in Christ Jesus.

Thank you for taking care of us. May we please you in everything and live for you in every moment. Amen.

20

When He's Rejected

You have heard that it was said, "Love your neighbor and hate your enemy." But I tell you, love your enemies and pray for those who persecute you, that you may be children of your Father in heaven. He causes his sun to rise on the evil and the good, and sends rain on the righteous and the unrighteous. If you love those who love you, what reward will you get? Are not even the tax collectors doing that? And if you greet only your own people, what are you doing more than others? Do not even pagans do that? Be perfect, therefore, as your heavenly Father is perfect.

Matthew 5:43–48

L ORD GOD,
    You know what it feels like to be hurt and rejected. You know the pain of being ignored, ridiculed, and wounded in the most horrifying ways. We read the story of Jesus's betrayal and death, and we grieve the injustice he suffered.

Because of that, I take comfort in knowing you relate to the hurt my son is going through. He may experience lies and gossip among his classmates. He may be left out when the boys are picking teams on the playground. The neighborhood friend he thought was loyal might decide he's too busy or mature to play with my son anymore. Someone may misunderstand him and react in anger, and my son may find himself alone. He may have to watch a reward that's rightfully his being given to someone else. People will disregard his property at times by damaging or losing it.

It seems too difficult to obey when you say to "love your enemies and pray for those who persecute you." But I do want to live as your child, and I long for my son to be your son as well. Give us the strength to put aside our selfish desires and give your grace to everyone in our lives.

Do your perfecting work in my son's heart. Guard him from keeping count of every wrong he suffers. Don't allow his mind to dwell on the ugly words of others, imagining the perfect sarcastic remark he could have spoken in return. Give him strength to forgive, whether the other person is sorry or not. Keep him from taking revenge in any form against those he considers his enemies.

Guard my heart so I never push my son away through my words or actions. It's impossible for him to be perfect, and I want to accept him as he is. He won't always measure up to my expectations, but I never want him to have to earn my love. May I give him grace, just as you give me, when he struggles or fails in any way. Make me faithful by your Spirit so he can see a glimpse of your perfect love and devotion in me.

Fill us with compassion for everyone. Show us how to reach out to others, no matter how unlovable or unlikable they are. And in this way, may we be your light in the world. Amen.

21

When He's Making Plans for the Future

Trust in the LORD with all your heart and lean not on your own understanding; in all your ways submit to him, and he will make your paths straight.

Proverbs 3:5–6

Therefore, I urge you, brothers and sisters, in view of God's mercy, to offer your bodies as a living sacrifice, holy and pleasing to God—this is your true and proper worship. Do not conform to the pattern of this world, but be transformed by the renewing of your mind. Then you will be able to test and approve what God's will is—his good, pleasing and perfect will.

Romans 12:1–2

LORD, I know that people's lives are not their own; it is not for them to direct their steps.

Jeremiah 10:23

LORD,
Thank you for the future you have in mind for my son. I hold to your promise that says, "I know the plans I have for you," declares the LORD, "plans to prosper you and not to harm you, plans to give

you hope and a future" (Jer. 29:11). Knowing my son is in your hands gives me peace and excitement about what's in store.

Give my son a heart that seeks your will for his life. So many possibilities are before him—new experiences and travel, education and career options, romance and friendships—he may become confused over which paths to take. Let him seek your will and your wisdom to know the way to go.

Guard my son from trusting in his own understanding. Let him seek wise counsel and the truth of your Word. Give him unshakeable faith to believe your ways and plans are perfect. May he accept even disappointment and failure as your opportunity to shape him into the man you want him to be.

Fill my son with devotion to you. May he worship by offering his life and dreams fully to your control. Give him strength to step away from the pattern of this world that pursues personal gain and success. Give him faith to "seek first his kingdom and his righteousness," believing that "all these things will be given to you as well" (Matt. 6:33).

Give me wisdom in how to encourage my son as he makes choices and plans. Show me how to support the development of the gifts and talents you've given. Let me seek your will for his life instead of pushing my own dreams or agenda for his future. Help me to value what *you* say as important, instead of pressuring him to achieve worldly success and achievement. May I value his character and righteousness beyond any trophies or honors he may receive.

Let us surrender our future to you. Give us joy in discovering your perfect will. May we walk faithfully before you until the day we see you face-to-face. Amen.

22

When He Has Work to Do

Whatever you do, work at it with all your heart, as working for the
Lord, not for human masters, since you know that you will receive
an inheritance from the Lord as a reward. It is the Lord Christ you
are serving.

Colossians 3:23–24

A lazy person craves food and there is none, but the appetite of hard-
working people is satisfied.

Proverbs 13:4 GW

Make it your ambition to lead a quiet life: you should mind your own
business and work with your hands, just as we told you, so that your
daily life may win the respect of outsiders and so that you will not be
dependent on anybody.

1 Thessalonians 4:11–12

L ORD,
     As my son grows in maturity his responsibilities increase as
well. He needs discipline to pursue his education, develop his skills,
grow in physical strength, and finish his chores for our household.
It's hard for him to resist the temptation to put his own fun ahead of
serving others and working with diligence.

Give my son eyes to see the value of work in his life. Give him a
sense of satisfaction for a job well done. Let him discover the truth
that he is serving you in everything he does, rather than just working
to please those around him.

Teach my son that his work today will bring rewards in the future. You promise him an inheritance as your servant. He will earn
the respect of others by his perseverance and integrity. He'll gain

independence through well-deserved income and not have to rely on others to care for him. He'll be able to follow the dreams of his heart without his own lack of motivation holding him back. Show my son that the temporary gratification of rest and relaxation will cost him the greater benefits of a job well done.

Give me wisdom to know how much responsibility my son can handle. It's easy to expect too little of him, which conveys a lack of confidence and hinders his growth. Yet I can also fall into demanding too much and discourage him in his efforts. Show me how I can provide opportunities to stretch him and help him grow, while not burdening him with unrealistic expectations. Let me show diligence in my own life so I can lead by example.

Thank you for all you're doing to equip my son for the future. Use the days while he's young to teach him the joy of working well. Give him understanding that "we are God's handiwork, created in Christ Jesus to do good works, which God prepared in advance for us to do" (Eph. 2:10). Fill him with a sense of purpose to accomplish all you have in store. Amen.

23

When He Needs Good Advice

The way of fools seems right to them, but the wise listen to advice.

Proverbs 12:15

Listen, my sons, to a father's instruction; pay attention and gain understanding. . . . Listen, my son, accept what I say, and the years of your life will be many. I instruct you in the way of wisdom and lead you along straight paths. When you walk, your steps will not be hampered; when you run, you will not stumble. Hold on to instruction, do not let it go; guard it well, for it is your life.

Proverbs 4:1, 10–13

FATHER,
My son is growing and becoming more independent. He likes to figure things out for himself. He doesn't always think things through and becomes frustrated when his plans fall apart. It's hard for him to slow down and take advice before he jumps into a new project. He tries to set his own goals and determine the road to achieve them, ignoring those who have more experience to share. His resistance to input and guidance is creating tension at home. He's hindering his success by refusing the help that's offered. He's having to learn life lessons the hard way, bringing unnecessary struggles and stress into his life.

Give my son humility to receive instruction and admit he doesn't know everything. Show him that parents and teachers are on his side. Help him to see that accepting help is not a sign of immaturity or weakness—it takes wisdom and strength to face our limitations. Fill him with a quiet spirit that can be still and listen. May he gain understanding so he can walk the path of life without stumbling.

Surround my son with excellent teachers. Give me and other adults in his life wisdom by your Spirit to know how to instruct my son. May he have discernment in choosing friends who show good judgment rather than foolishness. Let every influence and voice in his life encourage him to live by your truth.

Let my son learn to depend on your Word—the perfect source of wisdom and counsel. Keep him from pride that trusts in his own perceptions of how things should be. Give him ears to hear your truth and guide him in applying it to his life. Soften his heart to receive conviction when he's wrong. May he lean on you for strength to do what's right.

Thank you for being our source of perfect knowledge and wisdom. Let us seek your guidance in every situation and pursue your will in everything. Amen.

His Blessings

Give me neither poverty nor riches, but give me only my daily bread. Otherwise, I may have too much and disown you and say, "Who is the LORD?" Or I may become poor and steal, and so dishonor the name of my God.

Proverbs 30:8–9

I know what it is to be in need, and I know what it is to have plenty. I have learned the secret of being content in any and every situation, whether well fed or hungry, whether living in plenty or in want.

Philippians 4:12

As a parent living in a land of plenty, I want to be able to give my son good things. Just like Jesus said, "Which of you, if your son asks for bread, will give him a stone? Or if he asks for a fish, will give him a snake?" (Matt. 7:9–10). We know how to give our children what they need, whether it's a sack lunch on their way to school or a warm coat to wear on a chilly winter day. A parent's instinct to meet the needs of our children is an integral part of who God has made us to be.

We want our sons to have the best of everything. However, we often assume that the very best things for him are to make him comfortable and blessed. Of course I don't want a lazy child who sits around and waits for luxuries to be handed to him on a silver platter. But I do want him to have physical health so he can work and play hard. A strong mind to learn and succeed academically. Talents and gifts to develop and attain success. An attractive personality and social skills so he presents himself with confidence and is well liked. Sufficient income to maintain his household and enjoy the material things life has to offer.

Unfortunately, when I pray for all of these blessings it can contradict what God wants to do in my son's life. In his wisdom he may provide challenges, weaknesses, and loss to grow his faith and teach my son a greater dependence on him. Rob was recently visiting a friend who is battling cancer. She quoted the verse I mentioned above and said, "I think sometimes we're asking for the stone when we think we're asking for the bread." This friend went on to say how she was finding cancer to be God's bread for her. He was amazed to be sitting next to our dear friend as she sat on a hospital bed receiving chemotherapy treatment, saying joyfully that "this is God's bread for me!" Through the uncertainty of her illness, she was encountering God in powerful ways as he met her in the middle of her pain.

That is the kind of faith God desires all of his people to have, including our boys. I catch myself slipping into the kind of prayer that asks for a light and easy life for my son, believing I'm asking for "bread" for him. But God wants more than anything else to have a close, personal relationship with my son where he's trusted completely. If God answers every prayer of mine that asks for blessings, my son might become so consumed with enjoying the gifts that he leaves the giver behind. He may become caught up in pursuing his dreams instead of his Savior's face. He may confuse mere happiness with the true joy of satisfaction in God alone.

Rob remembers an experience where God's "bread" meant a challenging road for him. He moved around a lot when he was a kid. In sixth grade, after attending a different school for nearly each grade of his life, he decided he was done. He didn't want to invest in new friendships that he would have to move away from in a year or so. He stopped trying to connect with kids in his new class. He went home for lunch every day to avoid the kids in the cafeteria. As children tend to do, by distancing himself from other students and feeling sorry for himself, he allowed the whole situation to grow in his mind. He told himself that he didn't really need anyone, and the kids wouldn't want to get to know him anyway.

Of course this was very upsetting for his mom, seeing her young son isolating himself at home. Her mother's heart wanted to offer comfort and security by allowing him to keep coming home for lunch each day. But in her wisdom she could see how he really needed to stay at school at lunchtime and connect with other kids. She knew it was what it would take for him to grow and overcome his fears.

So one day she gave him lunch money and said he would not be coming home for lunch that day. He would be staying at school and eating in the lunchroom. He begged and cried, and told her she must hate him for making him stay at school. But she stayed strong and held her ground. She told him she wanted him to try having lunches at school for one week and they'd see what happened. Then I'm pretty sure she prayed her heart out over that lunch hour every day that week!

It didn't happen overnight, but that was the turning point for Rob to get over his fears and start meeting new kids. Once he crossed that hurdle it became one of the best school years he ever had. Keeping him at school was probably one of the hardest things his mom had ever asked him to do. It was hard on both of them, but letting him have his own way would have been far worse. Doing the hard thing turned out to be the most loving thing she could have done for him.

I'm slowly finding courage to pray that God would never bless my son in any area of his life if it will cost him closeness to his Savior. Sometimes I even have to pray that a reward or accomplishment is delayed so he can learn to wait and depend on God. There are times that achieving a trophy, an excellent grade, or a job promotion would be the worst thing that could happen, because it could stir up my son's pride and hinder his love for others.

Statistics show that even though we live in one of the most wealthy countries in the world, our nation has some of the highest rates of depression, suicide, and fear. It's obvious that money doesn't buy happiness! My son will only find true peace and satisfaction in the Lord. If he looks to find it in money, relationships, or success he'll always end up disappointed. God is big enough to take my son's loneliness, failures, and weaknesses and use them as blessings in his life if he keeps his trust in the Lord.

I need God's help to keep me from giving too much to my son, outside of God's best plans for him. He knows when my offers to help or pay his expenses will do him good or end up feeding a lazy or ungrateful attitude. It comes up in a myriad of ways every week—should he save his allowance for a movie ticket or should I open my wallet? Should I hover at his elbow while he works on a math assignment or let him push through on his own? Will a helping hand with raking the yard be an act of kindness or keep him from learning to stick with a job until it's done? Without the Spirit giving me discernment, I'll get in the way of what God is trying to teach him from day to day.

Life is too short to live just for our own pleasure. C. S. Lewis expressed it perfectly when he said, "If we consider the unblushing promises of reward and the staggering nature of the rewards promised in the Gospels, it would seem that Our Lord finds our desires not too strong, but too weak. We are half-hearted creatures, fooling about with drink and sex and ambition when infinite joy is offered us, like an ignorant child who wants to go on making mud pies in a slum because he cannot imagine what is meant by the offer of a holiday at the sea. We are far too easily pleased."[2]

May we find our greatest joy in life in walking with God, so all else pales by comparison. I pray that our son sees this kind of heart in his parents and discovers a heart fully satisfied by God alone.

24

When He Needs to Be Generous

They are to do good, to be rich in good works, to be generous and ready to share, thus storing up treasure for themselves as a good foundation for the future, so that they may take hold of that which is truly life.

1 Timothy 6:18–19 ESV

Remember this: Whoever sows sparingly will also reap sparingly, and whoever sows generously will also reap generously. Each of you should give what you have decided in your heart to give, not reluctantly or under compulsion, for God loves a cheerful giver. And God is able to bless you abundantly, so that in all things at all times, having all that you need, you will abound in every good work. As it is written: "They have freely scattered their gifts to the poor; their righteousness endures forever."

2 Corinthians 9:6–9

Lord,
It seems that one of the first words my child learned to speak was *mine!* Preschool play dates were spent encouraging him to share and take turns. I instructed my son to say thank you for his birthday and Christmas gifts, and to put coins in the collection buckets during the holidays. Year after year, I've encouraged generosity and gratitude at every opportunity, only to see his heart overcome by selfishness again.

Let my son see that his material possessions, his home, his family, his clothing, and his food are lavish gifts of love from your hand. May this awareness create gratitude, and may it develop deep compassion in his heart for those who are struggling. May he "sow generously" by giving cheerfully to those around him. May he "abound in every good work" by sharing what he has. Let him consider how he can bring happiness to others by his kindness and thoughtfulness.

When my son holds on tightly to what's his, he becomes jealous of the blessings of others. He wants to be first in line and receive the most attention. It frustrates him to have to wait for whatever he desires. Teach my son the mysterious truth that giving to others will bring amazing rewards. Any small loss he suffers now for the benefit of others will bring him a bountiful treasure and life in the end.

May my own life be marked by generosity. Let me give of my time and money for your name's sake. Let me show hospitality and actively look for ways to bless others. May my words be filled with gratitude and praise for the countless gifts you pour into my life each day.

Give us your compassion for the poor. Let our hearts be glad to give and share. Let us seek life in you rather than placing our hopes on gaining more and more for ourselves. Give us your heart of love for everyone, and use our generosity to shine your light in the darkness. Amen.

25

When He Hears False Teaching

Watch out for false prophets. They come to you in sheep's clothing, but inwardly they are ferocious wolves. By their fruit you will recognize them. Do people pick grapes from thornbushes, or figs from thistles? Likewise, every good tree bears good fruit, but a bad tree bears bad fruit.

Matthew 7:15–17

Remember your leaders, who spoke the word of God to you. Consider the outcome of their way of life and imitate their faith. Jesus Christ is the same yesterday and today and forever. Do not be carried away by all kinds of strange teachings.

Hebrews 13:7–9

So then, just as you received Christ Jesus as Lord, continue to live your lives in him, rooted and built up in him, strengthened in the faith as you were taught, and overflowing with thankfulness. See to it that no one takes you captive through hollow and deceptive philosophy, which depends on human tradition and the elemental spiritual forces of this world rather than on Christ.

Colossians 2:6–8

LORD,
The messages bombarding my son's mind every day are far from your truth. Our culture says that pursuing our individuality and gratification is the source of happiness. It says we can define marriage and family however we want to. That the created world came about by chance. That our value comes from pleasing people instead of you. That authority is to be mistrusted at best and blatantly disregarded at worst. That all roads lead to heaven, rather than the truth of Jesus—"I am the way and the truth and the life. No one comes to the Father except through me" (John 14:6).

Give my son discernment to recognize false teaching. Let him see how a person's beliefs are revealed by their actions. May his faith withstand any deception that could undermine his devotion to Christ. Give him courage to follow you even when he feels out of step with the world around him.

My son is surrounded by confusion and lies. Enable his mind to comprehend your gospel. May his faith be strengthened by the truth of your Word. May his spiritual life be rooted in Christ rather than superficial religious traditions. Give him gratitude for his salvation. Let him hold tightly to you when the world seems out of control.

May every word I speak to my son be true and right. Make me faithful in studying your Word and living by it in every way. Use me to encourage my son by living out a faith worth imitating.

Thank you for being our Rock. Even though the world's values and philosophies come and go, you never change. Keep us close and defend us from the lies of the enemy until you come again. Amen.

26

When He's Preparing for Marriage

Husbands, in the same way be considerate as you live with your wives, and treat them with respect as the weaker partner and as heirs with you of the gracious gift of life, so that nothing will hinder your prayers. Finally, all of you, be like-minded, be sympathetic, love one another, be compassionate and humble.

1 Peter 3:7–8

Do not be yoked together with unbelievers. For what do righteousness and wickedness have in common? Or what fellowship can light have with darkness? What harmony is there between Christ and Belial? Or what does a believer have in common with an unbeliever?

2 Corinthians 6:14–15

Husbands, love your wives, just as Christ loved the church and gave himself up for her.

Ephesians 5:25

LORD,
   You have said it is not good for man to be alone, but you would make a helper suitable for him (Gen. 2:18). I thank you for your

great love for my son that desires to someday bless him with a wife. Through her, you can bring encouragement, comfort, and support through every season of their life together.

I pray you would give my son wisdom when he's choosing his bride. Give him eyes to see past a girl's physical beauty, since "people look at the outward appearance, but the LORD looks at the heart" (1 Sam. 16:7). Teach him to value the inner character of his wife that will last for a lifetime. Let him treasure the "unfading beauty of a gentle and quiet spirit, which is of great worth in God's sight" (1 Pet. 3:4).

Build my son's courage and strength so he will be able to protect and serve his wife in every situation. Make him a peacemaker, quick to forgive and patient with her weaknesses. Give him a spirit of humility that can admit when he's wrong and treat her as his equal.

Give my son and his wife a shared faith in you. Be the head of their household and let them follow you in obedience. Bind them together as one as they worship and grow in their knowledge of you. Use them to serve each other and your church in Jesus's name.

Show me how to encourage my son in his marriage. Keep me from any jealousy of his devotion to his wife. Help me to give them my full blessing in establishing their own traditions, dreams, and decisions. Let everything I say and do promote their unity and happiness, and may they feel well loved in every way.

Give my son patience to wait for just the right partner you have in mind. Let him be content in his singleness and allow you to have authority over his future. Help him and his bride to guard their hearts, saving their emotional attachments and physical intimacy for each other. May they enter into their marriage free from scars, regrets, and baggage that will steal their joy and confidence in each other.

Thank you for the love you will show my son through his wife. Fill me with grace, wisdom, and love for my son until the day he says "I do." Amen.

27

When He's Having Fun

Finally, brothers and sisters, whatever is true, whatever is noble, whatever is right, whatever is pure, whatever is lovely, whatever is admirable—if anything is excellent or praiseworthy—think about such things. Whatever you have learned or received or heard from me, or seen in me—put it into practice. And the God of peace will be with you.

Philippians 4:8–9

I will be careful to lead a blameless life—when will you come to me? I will conduct the affairs of my house with a blameless heart. I will not look with approval on anything that is vile. I hate what faithless people do; I will have no part in it. The perverse of heart shall be far from me; I will have nothing to do with what is evil.

Psalm 101:2–4

And whatever you do, whether in word or deed, do it all in the name of the Lord Jesus, giving thanks to God the Father through him.

Colossians 3:17

FATHER,
We live in an environment with nearly limitless ways to relax and have a good time. My son can watch movies, play video games, compete in sports, enjoy the great outdoors, go to concerts, and hang out with friends. Store shelves are filled with toys, treats, and books, and our electronic devices can download countless apps and entertainment to view.

Thank you for creating a world with so much to enjoy. You know we can become weary from stress and the demands of our work, and you provide times of relaxation to build us up again. You've blessed our family with the means to make memories of good times together. We find laughter and enjoyment from the experiences you allow us to share.

Help my son to live for you even when he's having fun. Give him self-control to turn away from any images in movies, video games, or the internet that would steal his innocence. Never let him become desensitized to violence or evil that's present in so much of the entertainment today. Let him keep his mind pure so he can lead a blameless life.

Teach my son discipline in how he spends his time. Don't allow the toys or activities at his fingertips to distract him from his responsibilities. Make him faithful so that a job well done brings just as much joy as time spent playing.

Give me wisdom to know how to encourage him in his work and in finding good, clean fun. Show me how to protect him from "what faithless people do" that would cause my son to stumble. Show me how to provide the kinds of play that will make him stronger both mentally and physically. Make our home a place where we love your ways and seek to please you in everything we watch, hear, read, and do.

Thank you for showing us how we should live. May we submit our work and play to your control. Amen.

A Prayer Story

It's the hardest thing I've ever had to do as a parent: wait.

And that seems like the answer that God always gives me when I'm praying for my son, Justen. *Wait.*

When he was having health issues as a little boy, and doctors couldn't tell us what the issue was for years, the answer to our prayers was *wait*.

When he was sullen and moody as a teen, God's answer was *wait*.

And when we realized that those moods were more than a passing issue, when we realized that Justen needed real help, and it took not weeks or months but years to get him where he needed to be, the answer again was *wait*.

When Justen was nineteen, we were having huge issues of respect in our house. He wasn't helping with the basic chores around our place and had a horrible attitude. This hit me hard because I was on deadline for a writing project and I desperately wanted everyone to just "get along" while I was under so much pressure.

I told God I could handle the book deadline and Justen, but nothing else.

That's when I got a call from my mom.

She stated it plainly: she had cancer.

And I thought, *I can't handle this, God*.

And God said, *Wait*.

And as I planned and strategized of how I was going to help Justen, be with my mom, and finish my book, I started to panic. It was all too much and it was all up to me. And then I came down with whooping cough.

And that's when I finally had to admit that it wasn't going to happen. I couldn't fix Justen, I couldn't write, I couldn't take care of my mom. All I could do was ask God why, cry, and wait.

In the midst of the hardest time of my life, I was helpless. I felt alone and desperate. But God had not forgotten me.

In what seemed like the hundredth conversation with Justen about his life and his plans, and our frustrations and everything that was going on in our lives, he looked at me and said, "Why don't I go take care of Grandma?"

I honestly couldn't believe what I was hearing. Justen, who hadn't been able to see beyond himself in years, saw that I was sinking, saw that his grandmother needed him, and went outside of himself to offer help.

Suddenly, I was overwhelmed with hope—hope that God hears my cries and answers me. Hope that my mom would be cared for, and that I would have time to heal. And hope that the person Justen was really meant to be was buried deep inside him, struggling to come out.

In all the waiting and praying, God kept showing himself faithful. Even though it looked like nothing I had hoped or imagined, God knew what it would take to get a hold on Justen's heart.

Justen is now twenty-three. Every day we see signs of healing going on in his life, but sometimes it's not fast enough for his parents. And that's when I remember where we've been and all God has done, and remind myself that God does his greatest work in my son—and in me—when I remember to wait.

Kathi Lipp is the author of *Praying God's Word for Your Husband* and *Praying God's Word for Your Life*. She is a busy conference and retreat speaker who reaches thousands of women each year. She has been a guest on numerous national radio programs, including *Focus on the Family*. She and her husband have four children and live in California. Learn more at www.kathilipp.com.

28

When He Has Something to Say

We all stumble in many ways. Anyone who is never at fault in what they say is perfect, able to keep their whole body in check.

James 3:2

A good man brings good things out of the good stored up in his heart, and an evil man brings evil things out of the evil stored up in his heart. For the mouth speaks what the heart is full of.

Luke 6:45

Those who guard their lips preserve their lives, but those who speak rashly will come to ruin.

Proverbs 13:3

Do not let any unwholesome talk come out of your mouths, but only what is helpful for building others up according to their needs, that it may benefit those who listen.

Ephesians 4:29

FATHER,
    Thank you for the ways my son can express himself through his words. It feels so good to hear "I love you" and "thanks" for the ways I help him each day. His laughter and jokes make me smile. I feel proud when he shares a story of what he's learned or accomplished. You allow me to speak words of truth and encouragement into his life. We're able to speak to you about anything on our hearts through prayer. Through our words, you bind us closely to each other and to you.

However, there are many times when we tear each other down. I can be critical and harsh when I'm angry. He can become disrespectful and argue. I've embarrassed him by how I speak of him to others. Dishonest words can break down trust between us. As much as we love one another, we hurt each other's hearts by how we speak.

Help my son to use his words for good and not for evil. Give him self-control to be quiet before insults, sarcasm, or complaints are spoken. Make him a person of integrity who speaks the truth instead of telling lies or exaggerating. Fill his conversation with affirmation and encouragement to build others up. Enable him to articulate his feelings, ideas, and questions so he can be understood.

Fill my son's heart with your truth. Help him to remember who he is in you, so words of insecurity or self-hatred are silenced. Give him your love for others so he's not tempted to gossip or make fun of anyone. Store up your goodness in his heart, since "the mouth speaks what the heart is full of."

May my son's self-control over his tongue bring discipline to his life as well. Give him maturity beyond his years to master his impulses and live by your Spirit. Use my son as a light in the darkness as he speaks words of truth and grace to everyone. Amen.

29

When He Needs Self-Control

Like a city whose walls are broken through is a person who lacks self-control.

Proverbs 25:28

For the grace of God has appeared that offers salvation to all people. It teaches us to say "No" to ungodliness and worldly passions, and to live self-controlled, upright and godly lives in this present age, while we wait for the blessed hope—the appearing of the glory of our great God and Savior, Jesus Christ, who gave himself for us to redeem us from all wickedness and to purify for himself a people that are his very own, eager to do what is good.

Titus 2:11–14

LORD,
     While my son is a child he needs to be guided and governed in nearly every aspect of his life. His school schedule and bedtimes are dictated to him. He's instructed in what to eat and how to dress.

Homework and chores are assigned outside of his control. His freedom is limited by those in authority over him. In his immaturity as a child he needs others to set limits and boundaries for his own well-being.

As he grows, however, he'll take more and more responsibility for his decisions and behavior. He'll have to manage his life on his own, deciding when to work or sleep, whether or not to eat right and exercise, and who he'll spend time with. Without wisdom and self-control he may find himself falling into foolish habits and sin that bring destruction into his life.

Give my son strength to live an "upright and godly [life] in this present age." Keep him from being ruled by his emotions—keep anger, lust, impatience, and fear from taking over. When he's having a good time with friends, don't let him get carried away and find himself in risky situations that endanger his safety or reputation. When he gets behind the wheel, give him patience and focus to drive safely and follow the law. Energize him to work hard and discipline his time even when he's tempted to procrastinate. Let him have a protective, godly heart toward any girl he dates so he can preserve their purity and keep you first in his life.

Help my son to surrender his own will to yours. Give him self-control to obey those in authority even when he may not agree or understand. Let him think before he speaks and consider the outcome of his actions before he takes a step. Guard his heart from loving what the world loves, so he's not driven by a selfish desire for money, popularity, or success.

Let him put his passion into seeking you. Give him a love for your Word and your church. Give him the example of men who follow you with purpose and strength. Make him eager for your appearance so he lives in anticipation of seeing you face-to-face. Build him up so he can resist sin and do the right thing in every situation.

Thank you for giving your Spirit who purifies our hearts and equips us to live faithfully for you. Amen.

30

When He Needs to Confess

If we claim to be without sin, we deceive ourselves and the truth is not in us. If we confess our sins, he is faithful and just and will forgive us our sins and purify us from all unrighteousness.

1 John 1:8–9

Blessed is the one whose transgressions are forgiven, whose sins are covered. Blessed is the one whose sin the LORD does not count against them and in whose spirit is no deceit. When I kept silent, my bones wasted away through my groaning all day long. For day and night your hand was heavy on me; my strength was sapped as in the heat of summer. Then I acknowledged my sin to you and did not cover up my iniquity. I said, "I will confess my transgressions to the LORD." And you forgave the guilt of my sin.

Psalm 32:1–5

L ORD,
I can see the signs in my son when his conscience is troubling him. He avoids making eye contact. He's vague in his answers to questions. He seems distracted and keeps me at arm's length. As much as I regret the distance between us, it grieves me more that secret sins create a breach in his relationship with you.

Speak to my son's heart by your Spirit. Create sorrow and remorse over what he has done. Keep him from peace or rest until he's confessed his sin to me and to you. Give him courage to take responsibility for his actions. Enable him to do the work of making things right with anyone he has wronged.

Guard my son from blaming others for his mistakes. Give him humility to fully acknowledge his weaknesses and failures. Fill his heart with empathy to understand how his words and choices impact those around him. Make him eager to restore his relationship with you and others who care for him.

Prepare my heart to hear his confession. Make me "slow to speak and slow to become angry" (James 1:19). Just as you are faithful to forgive, give me compassion and patience so I can offer him forgiveness as well. Use my response to reveal your heart of love to my son.

Use this difficulty to bring us closer to each other and to you. Teach my son that honesty and humility bring peace and joy in his relationships. Build his faith so he will run to you with any burden he carries. Help him to live in your light instead of holding on to secrets in the dark.

Give my son the blessing of a clean heart. May he grow in his devotion to Christ as he experiences your mercy. Purify us in all things. Amen.

31

When He Needs Healing

Do you not know? Have you not heard? The LORD is the everlasting God, the Creator of the ends of the earth. He will not grow tired or weary, and his understanding no one can fathom. He gives strength to the weary and increases the power of the weak. Even youths grow tired and weary, and young men stumble and fall; but those who hope in the LORD will renew their strength. They will soar on wings like eagles; they will run and not grow weary, they will walk and not be faint.

Isaiah 40:28–31

Praise the LORD, my soul; all my inmost being, praise his holy name. Praise the LORD, my soul, and forget not all his benefits—who forgives all your sins and heals all your diseases, who redeems your life from the pit and crowns you with love and compassion, who satisfies your desires with good things so that your youth is renewed like the eagle's.

Psalm 103:1–5

F ATHER,
It's painfully hard to see my son suffering, whether he's sick in body or sick at heart. I would gladly take his hurt upon myself. He's weary and discouraged. He doesn't understand why he has to go through this, and I don't have the answers.

I pray that you would heal my son out of your love and mercy. He needs your strength and power to overcome his weakness. Restore his energy, his health, and his hope. Let him discover the reality of you as healer and redeemer by the way you restore his body and spirit.

Use this pain to increase my son's faith in you. Let him trust that you're present with him and in full control of his life. May he put his hope fully in you, believing you will "satisfy [his] desires with good things." Help him to accept your will—that you have allowed him to suffer—by knowing that "in all things God works for the good of those who love him, who have been called according to his purpose" (Rom. 8:28). You can use every trial to draw him closer to you and make him more like Jesus.

Help me to release my son to you. I fall into worry and doubt instead of trusting you to care for him. It's tempting to try to heal him by my own power. I can place my confidence in human wisdom or medical providers rather than you. Help me to remember that while you work through the hands of men, you are the ultimate Healer of all that is broken.

May we remember that our hearts need you even more than our physical bodies. You are our redeemer, and forgiveness is found in you. You give us hope of an eternal life with you, where you "will wipe every tear from [our] eyes. There will be no more death or mourning or crying or pain, for the old order of things has passed away" (Rev. 21:4). Give us patience to wait for your perfect healing. Amen.

32

When His Faith Is Shaken

Yet he did not waver through unbelief regarding the promise of God, but was strengthened in his faith and gave glory to God, being fully persuaded that God had power to do what he had promised.

Romans 4:20–21

Therefore we do not lose heart. Though outwardly we are wasting away, yet inwardly we are being renewed day by day. For our light and momentary troubles are achieving for us an eternal glory that far outweighs them all. So we fix our eyes not on what is seen, but on what is unseen, since what is seen is temporary, but what is unseen is eternal.

2 Corinthians 4:16–18

I pray that out of his glorious riches he may strengthen you with power through his Spirit in your inner being, so that Christ may dwell in your hearts through faith.

Ephesians 3:16–17

FATHER,
     This world is a broken place. We see the destruction of natural disasters, pain and death from disease, families broken by betrayal and divorce, cruel poverty, and violent crimes. There is nowhere to hide from tragedy—trouble will find us no matter how we pursue safety and peace.

As my son becomes more aware of evil and sorrow in this world, it is shaking his trust in you. He's asking the hard question of why a loving God allows terrible things to happen to innocent people. He's confused about why he experiences problems and disappointment even when he tries to do the right thing. The world that he can see with his eyes seems more real and powerful than an invisible God.

Strengthen my son's faith so he can hold on to belief in your promises. Don't let him lose heart, but trust that the struggles he's facing right now are only temporary. Replace his doubt with confidence, his hurt with comfort, and his confusion with clarity as he sets his eyes on you.

Let my son trust that you are truly in control. Help him to believe that you have not turned away from this world, for "the Lord is not slow in keeping his promise, as some understand slowness. Instead he is patient with you, not wanting anyone to perish, but everyone to come to repentance" (2 Pet. 3:9). Reassure him with the hope that "in keeping with his promise we are looking forward to a new heaven and a new earth, where righteousness dwells" (v. 13). No matter how dark things seem today, your plans for this world are perfect and you are coming to make all things new.

Show him how you never waste our pain. You use every hardship to shape us into Christ's image and draw us closer to you. Give him power through your Spirit to hold on to faith without wavering through unbelief.

Use me as a voice of hope and encouragement to my son. Make me steadfast, trusting and praising you in every situation. Show me how to share your Word so he can stand on your truth.

Thank you for helping us to hang on today, able to wait for our future with you in glory forever. Amen.

His Failures

For the righteous falls seven times and rises again, but the wicked stumble in times of calamity.

Proverbs 24:16 ESV

But he said to me, "My grace is sufficient for you, for my power is made perfect in weakness." Therefore I will boast all the more gladly about my weaknesses, so that Christ's power may rest on me. That is why, for Christ's sake, I delight in weaknesses, in insults, in hardships, in persecutions, in difficulties. For when I am weak, then I am strong.

2 Corinthians 12:9–10

Sum up the life of Jesus by any other standard than God's, and it is an anticlimax of failure.

Oswald Chambers[3]

The fear of failure can be as much of a driving force for our sons as the hope of success. It's tempting for them to find their identity in achievements and trophies, so failure means not just the loss of a dream but the loss of their sense of self. As parents, one of the greatest things we can teach our sons is that failure doesn't have to be a tragedy—it is actually an opportunity to experience the power of God in their life.

There is intense pressure put on our boys to succeed on every front. They feel they have to make the team, get the part, make the grade, attend the most prestigious college, attain a successful career, attract a desirable woman, and keep a brave face in every situation. They can put so much pressure on themselves to have it all that they'll fight for it at any cost—even if that means sacrificing their relationships with loved ones and God himself.

We can model this overachieving attitude in our lives as parents. We seem unable to say no when we're asked to help coach our son's team or provide dozens of cookies for every bake sale. We bring home extra work from the office to please an overbearing boss. We spend hours hand-sewing costumes because store-bought just isn't good enough. We can believe that disappointing others or considering our own health and well-being equals failure. This communicates to our sons that propping up our image is more important than seeking God's will for how we spend our time and energy.

What are the signs that our sons are afraid to fail? Does he use words like "loser" or "idiot" to describe himself? Does he get angry when he's put in a situation where he's weak or inexperienced? Is he critical of the weaknesses of others, indicating he's measuring their value by their performance? Has he "checked out," refusing to try new things or open himself up to new friendships? Maybe he's decided to stop studying or quit the team, so he doesn't have to say that he tried but failed in the end. Our sons' words and choices can tell us a lot about what's going on in their hearts.

There is hope for our boys because we serve a God who uses every difficulty—even failure—to do us good and bring us closer to himself. We need to let our boys know a few things. First, failure is universal. "For all have sinned and fall short of the glory of God" (Rom. 3:23). Every person on the planet will betray his or her own conscience and do the wrong thing. We can't hope for perfection until Jesus returns and completes his work of making us new. Until then, we need to let our sons know they will always find forgiveness with us and the Lord. Our prayer should be that our sons will take hold of the truth that "there is now no condemnation for those who are in Christ Jesus" (8:1).

The second thing to teach our sons is that failure is never wasted. God promises to take every situation and work it "for the good of those who love him, who have been called according to his purpose" (v. 28). Sometimes we really do learn the most the hard way! Losing an important homework assignment in his mess of a room can teach a better lesson than our nagging him to stay organized. Missing a friend's birthday party because he's sick can speak louder than we can about the benefits of eating right and getting enough sleep. Paying off a speeding ticket and the higher insurance premiums that follow can teach self-control and obedience. God wants to use our sons' mistakes to bring them to greater wisdom and maturity.

Third, our sons need to know that we're not going to rescue them from every failure. Our natural empathy as parents can make it hard for us to let them feel any pain. If we "help" him finish a book report by taking over and writing it ourselves, we're compromising our integrity and hindering his education. If we open our checkbook to cover the cost when he loses a library book or maxes out his data limit, we're keeping him from learning responsibility. If we try to influence the coach for a place on the team even though he didn't pass the tryouts, we're fostering a selfish sense of entitlement. We need to get out of the way sometimes, so God can use his failures to grow him into the man he intends him to be.

Finally, it is in our failure that we experience God's love and strength in our lives. When we reach a point of weakness where we just don't have what it takes, we can run to God for help. When our sons discover how close he is to them, and how God shows up when they're tired or in trouble, it will deepen their trust. It will take their faith from just believing *about* God to experiencing him personally in their lives.

Sometimes God allows failure to shine his light on the ugly places in our hearts. There's nothing like failure to show us our pride, jealousy, and misplaced priorities. It shows what we're depending on for our strength and value. It shows what we believe about love—is it a free gift from God or something to be earned? It reveals the true nature of our sons' relationship with his parents when we show patience and understanding or anger and criticism.

I don't love my sons because they're amazing (although I think they are!). I love them because they're mine. God doesn't love my children or me because we're perfect. He loves us because we're his chosen people, created to be with him forever. May we give our sons grace to fail without the fear of losing our hearts. And through our unconditional love, may they develop deeper faith in the unfailing love of their heavenly Father.

33

When He Needs Discipline

A rod and a reprimand impart wisdom, but a child left undisciplined disgraces its mother. . . . Discipline your children, and they will give you peace; they will bring you the delights you desire.

Proverbs 29:15, 17

Train up a child in the way he should go; even when he is old he will not depart from it.

Proverbs 22:6 ESV

Moreover, we have all had human fathers who disciplined us and we respected them for it. How much more should we submit to the Father of spirits and live! They disciplined us for a little while as they thought best; but God disciplines us for our good, in order that we may share in his holiness. No discipline seems pleasant at the time, but painful. Later on, however, it produces a harvest of righteousness and peace for those who have been trained by it.

Hebrews 12:9–11

FATHER,
I thank you that out of your great love, you correct and discipline me when I wander away from you. Every boundary and instruction in your Word is for my good. You are faithful to teach me your ways and rescue me from my own foolishness.

Just as you are bringing me to maturity by your Word and your Spirit, you have given me the responsibility of training my son. I am to teach him what is right and wrong, to obey you and the authority in his life, and the rewards and consequences of his decisions. I am to discipline him in love, to guard him from sin or weaknesses that will become a hindrance in his life.

I confess that I can resist the work of training and correcting my son. It's difficult to stand firm when he argues and complains. I become confused about what's true in different situations when he makes excuses or denies what he's done. I don't always trust my own discernment to understand his behavior or how to respond. Sometimes it's just easier to avoid conflict and the hard work of holding him accountable.

To neglect my son by letting him go his own way would be disobedience in my life as a parent. Failing to teach him your ways will open the door to trouble and hardship. Give me courage to set clear limits and expectations for his behavior. Make me faithful to teach him your Word and set an example of godliness. Give me strength to stand firm in my discipline, no matter whether he resists or receives it willingly. Remind me continually by your Spirit that correcting and disciplining my child is an expression of love and care.

Help me to respond to my son's mistakes with love rather than anger. Show me how to set rules based on your truth instead of my own convenience or preferences. Make me fair, gentle, and sensitive even when I have to be firm. May the goal always be to teach and restore—never to punish and shame.

Let my son experience your love through me as I guide and teach him to follow you. Help me to parent him in wisdom and love in every situation. Amen.

34

When His Life Is Changing

Jesus Christ is the same yesterday and today and forever.

Hebrews 13:8

There is a time for everything, and a season for every activity under the heavens: a time to be born and a time to die, a time to plant and a time to uproot, a time to kill and a time to heal, a time to tear down and a time to build, a time to weep and a time to laugh, a time to mourn and a time to dance, a time to scatter stones and a time to gather them, a time to embrace and a time to refrain from embracing, a time to search and a time to give up, a time to keep and a time to throw away, a time to tear and a time to mend, a time to be silent and a time to speak, a time to love and a time to hate, a time for war and a time for peace.

Ecclesiastes 3:1–8

The steadfast love of the LORD never ceases; his mercies never come to an end; they are new every morning.

Lamentations 3:22–23 ESV

FATHER,
    Thank you for being our God who never changes. No matter how unstable or unpredictable our circumstances may feel, we can rest securely in you. I don't have to fear the future because you "set my feet on a rock and gave me a firm place to stand" (Ps. 40:2).

My son faces changes in his life both today and in the future. He'll experience new classrooms, employment, relationships, and challenges. His body will develop into adulthood. He'll suffer the loss of people and possessions he depended on. New opportunities will test his courage and abilities. In each situation, he'll be torn between excitement and anxiety.

Let my son find peace in knowing you are the author of his life story. He can be sure that wherever he goes and whatever happens, you will be with him. Let him rejoice like David, able to say, "If I go up to the heavens, you are there; if I make my bed in the depths, you are there. If I rise on the wings of the dawn, if I settle on the far side of the sea, even there your hand will guide me, your right hand will hold me fast" (139:8–10). May he find courage to face every circumstance by knowing you will never leave his side.

Enable my son to accept where he is right now. Let him recognize that you intend to use everything that happens, whether difficult or wonderful, to reveal yourself and mold him into the man you want him to be. Let him be content, rather than trying to avoid this new challenge or rush ahead of your timing. May he surrender his will and his plans to your perfect control.

Use me to encourage him in trusting you. Fill my words with messages of hope for the future and gratitude for your gifts to us today. Make me patient and full of faith, so I can offer him the security of a peaceful, steadfast parent.

Thank you for your constant love and presence wherever we go. You are our hope and our peace. Amen.

35

When He's Forming His Identity

Do not love the world or anything in the world. If anyone loves the world, love for the Father is not in them. For everything in the world—the lust of the flesh, the lust of the eyes, and the pride of life—comes not from the Father but from the world. The world and its desires pass away, but whoever does the will of God lives forever.

1 John 2:15–17

But you are a chosen people, a royal priesthood, a holy nation, God's special possession, that you may declare the praises of him who called you out of darkness into his wonderful light.

1 Peter 2:9

For he chose us in him before the creation of the world to be holy
and blameless in his sight. In love he predestined us for adoption to
sonship through Jesus Christ, in accordance with his pleasure and
will—to the praise of his glorious grace, which he has freely given us
in the One he loves.

Ephesians 1:4–6

L ORD,
It is miraculous that in you we find an entirely new identity.
You call us your adopted children. Chosen. Holy. Blameless. A new
creation. Beloved. You know our every thought and chose us before
the creation of the world to be yours. We are set free from the power
of sin and given the promise of eternity with you.

Despite your many promises that we are yours forever, we can
find ourselves confused about who we really are. The world says our
identity is found in our appearance and achievements. Happiness is
promised through fame and material possessions. Humility, purity,
and faith in Jesus are considered foolish and worthless.

Give my son the knowledge of who he truly is as your child. Let
him acknowledge you as his Creator and King. Let his heart love you
instead of this broken world. Help him to escape the lies and temptations that will take his eyes from you and lead him into darkness.

Guard my son from the temptation to look for happiness and
satisfaction in what the world can offer. Keep him from a false sense
of importance based on his looks, talents, and financial success. Help
him to find your will and follow you rather than seeking his destiny
on his own.

Use me to declare the truth of who he is as your child. May I affirm his inner character more than his outward accomplishments.
Let me value his clean heart over his handsome appearance. Help me
to encourage his obedience to you rather than his performance for
others. Keep us focused on preparing for eternity with you, placing
your kingdom above any earthly goal or desire.

Thank you for calling us into your light. Our hope and salvation are found only in you. You've given us the real purpose for living each day. May we praise you forever. Amen.

36

When He Needs a Christian Community

Two are better than one, because they have a good return for their labor: If either of them falls down, one can help the other up. But pity anyone who falls and has no one to help them up. Also, if two lie down together, they will keep warm. But how can one keep warm alone? Though one may be overpowered, two can defend themselves. A cord of three strands is not quickly broken.

Ecclesiastes 4:9–12

Above all, love each other deeply, because love covers over a multitude of sins. Offer hospitality to one another without grumbling. Each of you should use whatever gift you have received to serve others, as faithful stewards of God's grace in its various forms. If anyone speaks, they should do so as one who speaks the very words of God. If anyone serves, they should do so with the strength God provides, so that in all things God may be praised through Jesus Christ. To him be the glory and the power for ever and ever. Amen.

1 Peter 4:8–11

And let us consider how we may spur one another on toward love and good deeds, not giving up meeting together, as some are in the habit of doing, but encouraging one another—and all the more as you see the Day approaching.

Hebrews 10:24–25

FATHER,
    Thank you for building your church so we don't have to walk the path of faith alone. You have given us brothers and sisters in Christ to build us up when we're discouraged. We discover the truth of your Word through pastors and teachers. When we're sick or experiencing hardship, we find prayer and help when we need them most. I pray that my son would experience the gift of the family of God.

Surround my son with Christians who will challenge him to stay faithful to you. Provide teachers who will open the Word in a way that captures his heart and mind. Let godly men live before him as examples of obedience as he grows. Make your people his strongest advocates, leaders, and friends.

Create a desire in my son's heart to fully participate in the life of the church. Let him discover joy in serving others with the gifts your Spirit provides. Make the body of Christ a community where he can be fully himself without pretending or performing for approval. Let his spiritual family be just as significant as his earthly family in loving and caring about him.

The people of God aren't perfect and will fail my son at times. Give him grace to forgive, and keep the failures of others from undermining his trust in your perfect holiness. May he give grace to his brothers and sisters when they stumble, and may he receive mercy in his weaknesses as well.

Let me set an example as his parent by my faithfulness to the body of Christ. Give me a servant's attitude that seeks to share my home, my gifts, and my time with your people. Make me diligent in leading my son to worship each week. Give me grace that seeks the good of others without criticism or negativity.

Reveal your great love and truth to my son through other believers in our lives. May we receive encouragement and help, and discover more of your goodness than we ever knew before. Amen.

A Prayer Story

For you created my inmost being; you knit me together in my mother's womb. I praise you because I am fearfully and wonderfully made; your works are wonderful, I know that full well.

Psalm 139:13–14

Ever feel at the end of yourself as a parent? Yeah, me too! One day, our then-eight-year-old son, Zach, came into the house from playing outside with his brothers, Brock and Caleb, who were in tears. He was beating on them again! Zach had a medical issue and a learning disability and wasn't very verbal, so when frustrated he used his fists.

"Zach," I bent down and whispered intently into his face, "you cannot do this. Hitting is inappropriate. Go upstairs and I will come up to talk to you."

Zach stomped up the stairs, knocking his brothers over in the process. He slammed the door to his room and threw a baseball at it, knocking a hole through the door as I walked in. I had bounded up the stairs just behind him, praying all the way up because I had made a commitment to never, ever discipline in anger. But I wasn't angry. I was scared, scared for my son.

I walked into the room, bent down so I was eye to eye with him and said firmly but calmly, "Zachery, this is inappropriate. I know you are angry. I know you are upset. But you cannot use your fists to show it. You have got to learn to use words to express your feelings."

(I was thinking, *If you act like this no one will ever marry you and you are going to live with me forever! Use words!*)

Zach exploded and yelled back at me, hands on his hips, "You want words! You want words! Then I hate myself and I hate my life and if God made me, I hate him too!"

I was filled with shocked silence. I simply replied in a whisper, "I'll be right back."

I ran to my room in tears. I threw myself across my bed and desperately prayed to God, "Lord, I am a pastor's wife, a director of women's ministry, and I write all these Christian books, and I am raising a little atheist upstairs—I need HELP! I am so afraid for Zachery. I don't know what to do. All I do know is that Psalm 139 says he is fearfully and wonderfully made. I believe that. I believe there is a gift, a treasure, that you place in each and every one of us. But God, Zach is so angry he cannot see the treasure—help me help him see that treasure!"

Then the idea came. I ran to the office and pulled out a piece of poster board. I drew a treasure map on it with a bunch of lines and a treasure chest at one end, glued a quarter or two onto the map, and marched myself back upstairs where Zach stood, just as I had left him.

"Zach, here's the deal. You and I are going to go on an adventure. See, God has placed a treasure, a special uniqueness inside every person. There is a treasure in you, Zach," I said as I tapped on his chest. "You and I and God are going on a treasure hunt to discover that hidden treasure. So here's the plan. I am going to ask you every day to name one positive thing about your day and one thing you think you did well. Then once a week, you and I are going on a breakfast date and we're going to talk about what we see God showing you about the treasure inside you. We're going to do this for at least six weeks and at the end of that time, I am going to invest money in the treasure God has shown is in you. Zach, you are a special guy. We all love you, and God loves you most of all. Let's ask God to help us discover your treasure. What's one positive thing that happened today? Let's write it down."

Zach had a chronic Eeyore-like attitude, so he said, "It's hopeless, it's never going to work."

I spoke for him, "Honey, you are alive." (I was holding back my own frustration because I was sarcastically thinking, *Yep, you are alive— because I haven't killed you from sheer frustration, kid!*) But God miraculously replaced my frustration with compassion, and I wrapped my arms around that sullen, stiff little body and whispered, "You are God's treasure!"

Then a miracle happened. Zach started bringing me the treasure map, too excited to list off all the great things he was seeing in himself. At the end of those six weeks, we discovered that relationships were the key to unlocking Zach's heart and hope, so we budgeted to provide him opportunities (concerts, camps, workshops, and so forth) to find friends to grow with God and make good decisions with.

Fast-forward to now, about seventeen years later. That same son graduated with a master's degree in exercise science (with honors) and was hired the day he graduated to be a strength coach for a Division I university. On June 22, he was married to a beautiful, godly woman who values the treasure of Zach! Miracles happen when you look for the treasure!

Lord, sometimes it is so hard to see the treasure in our kids, spouse, coworkers, or extended family members. Today, help me see people with your eyes—eyes that see the treasure you see in them.

Pam Farrel is an international speaker, the author of over thirty-eight books including *Men Are Like Waffles, Women Are Like Spaghetti*; *Brave New Woman*; and *52 Ways to Wow Your Husband*. She is the codirector of Love-Wise (www.Love-Wise.com) and the founder of Seasoned Sisters (www.seasonedsisters.com).

37

When He's Rebellious

Do not be like the horse or the mule, which have no understanding but must be controlled by bit and bridle or they will not come to you. Many are the woes of the wicked, but the LORD's unfailing love surrounds the one who trusts in him.

Psalm 32:9–10

But I gave them this command: Obey me, and I will be your God and you will be my people. Walk in obedience to all I command you, that it may go well with you. But they did not listen or pay attention; instead, they followed the stubborn inclinations of their evil hearts. They went backward and not forward.

Jeremiah 7:23–24

How can a young person stay on the path of purity? By living according to your word. I seek you with all my heart; do not let me stray from your commands. I have hidden your word in my heart that I might not sin against you. Praise be to you, LORD; teach me your decrees. With my lips I recount all the laws that come from your mouth. I rejoice in following your statutes as one rejoices in great riches. I meditate on your precepts and consider your ways. I delight in your decrees; I will not neglect your word.

Psalm 119:9–16

LORD,
My son is determined to have his own way. He resists authority. He thinks he's the only one who knows what's best for him. Rules make him angry, and he won't take no for an answer. When I try to reason with him or "lay down the law," he shuts down and rejects whatever I say.

Help my son to see that the freedom he's seeking will only bring him pain. The boundaries you set for us, and the limits I put in place, are meant for his well-being. If he persists in running his own life he'll only go "backward and not forward."

Give my son the humility to see that he needs you. Show him that true freedom and joy are found in trusting you and submitting to your will. Help him to understand your unfailing love that seeks only to do him good every day of his life.

Help my son to comprehend that self-control and obedience lead to greater independence in the end. As he earns trust and takes on responsibility for himself, he'll gain the esteem and confidence of others. Allow him to grow in his ability to govern himself so he won't need someone else to take control.

Give me wisdom to know when to take charge and when to let go. If I'm in error of being too controlling, show me what areas to release. If I'm avoiding the responsibility of taking authority over my son, give me courage to stand firm no matter how he responds or pressures me to give in. Above all, bring us to a place of trust and unity. Help me to hold on to hope and compassion for my son, and help him to believe my motives of love when I don't give him the freedom he's fighting for.

Above all, I pray my son would surrender himself to you. Be his Savior and his King. Let him say like the psalmist, "I have chosen the way of faithfulness; I have set my heart on your laws. I hold fast to your statutes, LORD; do not let me be put to shame. I run in the path of your commands, for you have broadened my understanding" (Ps. 119:30–32). Amen.

38

When He's Bored

This is the day that the LORD has made; let us rejoice and be glad in it.

Psalm 118:24 ESV

For we are God's handiwork, created in Christ Jesus to do good works, which God prepared in advance for us to do.

Ephesians 2:10

A person can do nothing better than to eat and drink and find satisfaction in their own toil. This too, I see, is from the hand of God, for without him, who can eat or find enjoyment? To the person who pleases him, God gives wisdom, knowledge and happiness.

Ecclesiastes 2:24–26

LORD,
You have given us many gifts in the form of meaningful work, good friends, hobbies and sports, and rest and relaxation. However, sometimes our routine becomes repetitive and my son craves a change of pace. As he feels restless and bored, he can lose his gratitude for the blessings in his life. His days lack purpose and his motivation disappears.

Use this season of boredom to teach my son to endure. Let him mature in the ability to work faithfully and with a positive attitude, without being sidelined by his emotions. Give him confidence that you're in control and will bring new opportunities and excitement at the perfect time. Let him be grateful for your gifts instead of dwelling on what he can't do or have today.

Let my son hear your voice during this quiet season in his life. Prompt him to pursue a deeper connection with you and our family.

Use these days as a time of rest to build him up for the greater challenges you're preparing for his future.

I pray that you would bring new relationships and experiences to my son. Use them to grow him into the man you've designed him to be. Develop courage, skill, and faith in you as he's led to try unfamiliar things. Help him to walk in both a spirit of contentment today and in joyful anticipation of where you'll lead him tomorrow.

Remind my son that each day is a gift from you. Let him wake each morning ready to discover your purpose for his time and energy. Give him eyes to see the good works you've prepared for him to do, and a willing attitude to serve and help the people you bring his way.

Keep us from squandering the quiet hours we're given—use them to teach us the art of being still and listening for your voice. Open our eyes to the ways you reveal your presence to us each day—keep us from missing the wonders of your creation, the ways you answer prayer, and the truth of your Word. In you, every moment has meaning and much to be grateful for.

May we praise you for every day we're given. Amen.

39

When He Goes Online

Be alert and of sober mind. Your enemy the devil prowls around like a roaring lion looking for someone to devour.

1 Peter 5:8

In his arrogance the wicked man hunts down the weak, who are caught in the schemes he devises . . . like a lion in cover he lies in wait. He lies in wait to catch the helpless; he catches the helpless and drags them off in his net. His victims are crushed, they collapse; they fall under his strength. He says to himself, "God will never notice; he covers his face and never sees."

Psalm 10:2, 9–11

Whoever dwells in the shelter of the Most High will rest in the shadow of the Almighty. I will say of the LORD, "He is my refuge and my fortress, my God, in whom I trust." Surely he will save you from the fowler's snare and from the deadly pestilence. He will cover you with his feathers, and under his wings you will find refuge; his faithfulness will be your shield and rampart.

Psalm 91:1–4

LORD,
You have used the internet to provide many blessings for our family. We enjoy the convenience of researching any topic easily, avoiding trips to the store with online shopping, managing our finances, and connecting with friends and loved ones far away. You are using it to open the way for the gospel in places around the globe it has never reached before.

However, as my son's world is able to expand by going online, he is at risk of harm as well. His innocence may be lost through exposure to pornography. Materialism and greed can take hold by the barrage of advertising displayed. Gossip and cyberbullying can create isolation and deep insecurity at school. Predators can seek to lure him into unthinkable sexual exploitation. My son needs your help and protection every time he goes online.

Give my son wisdom and self-control to handle the internet safely. Guard him from sharing personal information with strangers. Protect his eyes from any images that would steal his purity and innocence. Fill his heart with an aversion to violence and perversion. Give him strength to shut down and walk away from any site that could take his eyes off of you.

Use the internet to build his relationships rather than tear them down. Give him wisdom with every word he types and every video he posts, so no one is dishonored in any way. Protect him from anyone who would try to damage his reputation with hurtful lies or attacks.

Help my son to keep devices in their proper place in his life. May he balance his time wisely so his days are active and full, without being overtaken by countless hours in front of screens. Let him find his greatest satisfaction in his relationships and talents from you, instead of losing himself online.

Give me wisdom as his parent to know what safeguards and limits I should put in place. Show me how to make the internet the most positive, beneficial tool for him that it can be. Create an open relationship between us so he doesn't keep any online relationships or experiences a secret. May he have a submissive spirit to accept my input and authority over this area of his life.

Thank you that you're always with my son, whether he's down the street or exploring online. Guide him and keep him close to you every moment. Amen.

40

When He Feels Alone

The LORD himself goes before you and will be with you; he will never leave you nor forsake you. Do not be afraid; do not be discouraged.

Deuteronomy 31:8

And surely I am with you always, to the very end of the age.

Matthew 28:20

Where can I go from your Spirit? Where can I flee from your presence? If I go up to the heavens, you are there; if I make my bed in the depths, you are there. If I rise on the wings of the dawn, if I settle on the far side of the sea, even there your hand will guide me, your right hand will hold me fast.

Psalm 139:7–10

FATHER,
     There are times in our lives when we feel completely alone. We're the new kid at school or the newly hired employee who's trying to find where we fit in. Everyone at church has old, familiar friends while we feel invisible and out of place. The neighbors all know each other and share memories but don't even wave when we walk by. Other musicians or athletes are more experienced and team together, so we feel out of place as we work on basic skills. The feeling of not belonging is painful and embarrassing.

My son is discouraged and believes he's unseen and unwanted. His friendly efforts to reach out have been ignored. He feels inferior, doubting he has much to offer. He doesn't know what steps to take to make friends and find others with common interests. His insecurity is growing—he's beginning to give up, becoming quiet and withdrawn. He's building walls around his heart to defend against rejection.

I pray you would provide my son with friends. Give him a sense of belonging, and open others' eyes to see how valuable and special he truly is. May he receive acceptance and kindness from those around him each day.

It hurts to see my son in pain when I know he's loved completely by you and by me. Use this time of solitude to reveal yourself as his faithful friend. Let him discover the truth that you're with him every moment. Prompt him to talk to you in prayer and depend on you when he's struggling. May he discover such fulfillment in your presence that no earthly relationship could ever compare. Let him see you as the source of every good thing in his life. Help him to trust you'll bring the right companions at the perfect time.

Build our relationship with each other during this season. Show me how to reach out to him and make memories together. Give me sensitivity to when he needs some fun or attention the most. Keep me diligent in prayer over him, knowing you love him and have his life in your hands. Let my words be filled with encouragement and hope when he's doubting how much you care.

Thank you for being the source of everything good for my son. I praise you for your faithful hand of guidance and protection that keeps him secure. Thank you for your love that never lets him go. Amen.

41

When He Needs to Talk to God

In the same way, the Spirit helps us in our weakness. We do not know what we ought to pray for, but the Spirit himself intercedes for us through wordless groans.

Romans 8:26

I call on you, my God, for you will answer me; turn your ear to me and hear my prayer.

Psalm 17:6

Is anyone among you in trouble? Let them pray. Is anyone happy? Let them sing songs of praise. Is anyone among you sick? Let them call the elders of the church to pray over them and anoint them with oil in the name of the Lord. And the prayer offered in faith will make the sick person well; the Lord will raise them up. If they have sinned, they will be forgiven. Therefore confess your sins to each other and pray for each other so that you may be healed. The prayer of a righteous person is powerful and effective.

James 5:13–16

Rejoice always, pray continually, give thanks in all circumstances; for this is God's will for you in Christ Jesus.

1 Thessalonians 5:16–18

L ORD,
    Thank you for inviting us into your presence through prayer. You're ready to listen to every word of gratitude, concern, or confession that we bring before you. When we're hurting and too broken or confused to speak, your Spirit helps us and even prays on our behalf. When we bring our needs to you we find healing, help, and forgiveness. You bring joy to our hearts and fill us with praise.

I pray that my son will discover the gift of prayer for himself. Show him that it's more than merely saying grace before a meal or asking you to "bless Mom and Dad" before he falls asleep. Grow his faith to believe you really hear him when he speaks to you. Give him joyful expectancy that you'll respond. Let him learn to know your voice as you meet him on his knees.

Teach my son how to pray. Let him discover how close you are and how eager you are to receive him in prayer. Reveal your power by providing for the needs he brings before you. Let him learn gratitude by acknowledging you as the source of every good thing in his life. Bring peace to his heart as he finds forgiveness in you. Develop a compassionate spirit in him as he lifts up the burdens of others in prayer. Give him wisdom when he asks you which way to go. May his life be changed forever as he learns to speak with you in every situation.

Make me faithful in prayer as an example to my son. Let him see your peace and courage in me every time I look to you for help. Give me strength to pray continually, without becoming distracted by stress or a busy schedule. Give me a grateful heart that praises you in all circumstances.

Thank you for inviting us to pray. You enter into our troubles, happiness, sickness, and weakness every time we come to you. We never have to walk through life alone. You are faithful to listen and show us mercy. I praise your name for your perfect love. Amen.

42

When He Can Serve Others

Not so with you. Instead, whoever wants to become great among you must be your servant, and whoever wants to be first must be slave of all. For even the Son of Man did not come to be served, but to serve, and to give his life as a ransom for many.

Mark 10:43–45

Be devoted to one another in love. Honor one another above yourselves. Never be lacking in zeal, but keep your spiritual fervor, serving the Lord. Be joyful in hope, patient in affliction, faithful in prayer. Share with the Lord's people who are in need. Practice hospitality.

Romans 12:10–13

And do not forget to do good and to share with others, for with such sacrifices God is pleased.

Hebrews 13:16

FATHER,
You have given my son countless blessings through the service of people in his life. His teachers spend hour upon hour preparing lessons and helping him grow academically. Leaders at church invest time in sharing the Word and praying over his life. He's received fun experiences and a helping hand from friends who care for him. I

provide his meals and clothes, and I try to anticipate his needs before he even asks. My son is well cared for and loved.

I pray that you would fill my son with gratitude for all that others do for him each day. Open his eyes to understand the time, effort, and money required to meet his needs. Use this awareness to create a heart that's eager to serve as he's been served.

Let my son have a willing spirit to help within our home. Prompt him to carry in groceries from the car or take out the trash without being asked. Give him patience to do his chores without complaining or quitting before he's through. Let him know he's a significant member of the family—not merely a guest—who can find joy in giving of himself to our household.

Give my son opportunities to help others at school, at church, and in our neighborhood. Open his eyes to see what actions he could take to benefit his classroom and community. Move his heart to give his time and money for the needs of others. Make him sensitive to kids who are having a rough day and need a friend.

Guard my son's heart and mind from becoming self-focused. Let him see how his actions affect others. Show him what a powerful impact his kindness and generosity can have on the world around him. May he live as your light in the darkness as others see the love of Christ working through him.

Thank you for all the ways you give yourself to us. May we respond to your love by caring for everyone you bring into our lives. Amen.

43

When His Reputation Is at Stake

A good name is more desirable than great riches; to be esteemed is better than silver or gold.

Proverbs 22:1

Dear friends, I urge you, as foreigners and exiles, to abstain from sinful desires, which wage war against your soul. Live such good lives among the pagans that, though they accuse you of doing wrong, they may see your good deeds and glorify God on the day he visits us.

1 Peter 2:11–12

Let love and faithfulness never leave you; bind them around your neck, write them on the tablet of your heart. Then you will win favor and a good name in the sight of God and man.

Proverbs 3:3–4

FATHER,
You say that "even a child makes himself known by his acts, by whether his conduct is pure and upright" (Prov. 20:11 ESV). My son is discovering the reality of that truth, as his reputation is threatened by his own mistakes and the slander of others.

I pray you would uphold my son's reputation wherever he goes. Give him self-control so he's not labeled as a rowdy troublemaker. Give him respect and proper manners so he's appreciated by those in authority. Give him compassion and love for others, so he's known for his kind friendship and generosity. Let a desire to please you govern his words and his behavior in every situation.

Keep single offenses or mistakes from determining how others see him. I pray he would receive grace and second chances from people, just as we find mercy and love in you. If he is experiencing harmful gossip or insults, silence any lies and keep his good name intact. May he find rest in knowing your love is faithful even if everyone else turns away.

Let my son value his reputation. Help him to understand how easy it is to lose and how difficult it is to restore. Make him mindful of how impulsive words and foolish actions can follow him for ages. Guard him from texting or posting pictures or comments online that could impact his image. Help him to make mature decisions about his language, his appearance, the kids he chooses to hang out with, and his academic efforts.

I pray that my son would love you and seek your favor. May his outward behavior flow from an inward love and devotion to you. Teach him faithfulness and obedience. Keep him pure and give him wisdom to know what is right.

Let me love my son unconditionally so he never has to worry about losing my heart. May I have the kind of love for him that is patient, always hopes, and keeps no record of wrongs (1 Cor. 13). No matter what the world may say of him, may he always find acceptance with me.

Thank you for lifting us up when our sins bring us down. My son is in your hands—may he bring glory to your name as he lives for you. Amen.

44

When He Has Enemies

Be still before the LORD and wait patiently for him; do not fret when people succeed in their ways, when they carry out their wicked schemes. Refrain from anger and turn from wrath; do not fret—it leads only to evil. For those who are evil will be destroyed, but those who hope in the LORD will inherit the land. A little while, and the wicked will be no more; though you look for them, they will not be found. But the meek will inherit the land and enjoy peace and prosperity. The wicked plot against the righteous and gnash their teeth at them; but the Lord laughs at the wicked, for he knows their day is coming. The wicked draw the sword and bend the bow to bring down the poor and needy, to slay those whose ways are upright. But their swords will pierce their own hearts, and their bows will be broken.

Psalm 37:7–15

Love your enemies, do good to those who hate you, bless those who curse you, pray for those who mistreat you. If someone slaps you on one cheek, turn to them the other also. If someone takes your coat, do not withhold your shirt from them. Give to everyone who asks you, and if anyone takes what belongs to you, do not demand it back. Do to others as you would have them do to you.

Luke 6:27–31

LORD,
       You know the enemy my son is battling at this moment. He finds himself slandered, bullied, and intimidated. He's afraid of what he might lose—his safety, his reputation, and his self-respect. Those who ought to stand for him are either unaware of his needs or ineffective in their efforts to protect him. My son is feeling crushed and hopeless. He needs your help.

Give my son faith to believe you will deliver him out of this situation. May he be still and wait patiently for you to rescue him. He feels weak and embarrassed, frustrated and confused. Give him peace as he trusts in you. Let him be still and free from worry, with joyful anticipation that your power will be revealed at exactly the right time.

Fill my son with compassion by your Spirit so he can pray for his enemy and return good for evil. Free him from any desire for revenge. Let him depend on you to fight his battles so he doesn't engage in angry retaliation on his own. Make his words and behavior completely blameless so any attacks and accusations fall away to nothing. Uphold his reputation, that his kindness and self-control are regarded as strength. Give him courage to do the right thing no matter what comes against him each day.

Give me wisdom to know when to stand by and wait for you, and when to act on his behalf. Keep me from trying to protect my son through my own strength instead of yours. Show me how to encourage him to trust you. Give me a merciful attitude toward his enemies when I want to lash out and make them pay.

Give my son courage to talk about his pain. Show him who he can lean on and look to for support. Keep him from carrying his burden in secret to avoid embarrassment or further abuse from his enemies. Create opportunities for him to show grace and kindness, for "If your enemy is hungry, give him food to eat; if he is thirsty, give him water to drink. In doing this, you will heap burning coals on his head, and the LORD will reward you" (Prov. 25:21–22). Let him discover your reward for having integrity in this hard situation.

Thank you for watching over him in every moment. I release my son fully to you, trusting in your strength and protection rather than my own. Thank you for your great love that never fails. Amen.

45

When He Can Share the Gospel

You are the light of the world. A town built on a hill cannot be hidden. Neither do people light a lamp and put it under a bowl. Instead they put it on its stand, and it gives light to everyone in the house.

In the same way, let your light shine before others, that they may see your good deeds and glorify your Father in heaven.

Matthew 5:14–16

But in your hearts revere Christ as Lord. Always be prepared to give an answer to everyone who asks you to give the reason for the hope that you have.

1 Peter 3:15

I am not ashamed of the gospel, because it is the power of God that brings salvation to everyone who believes: first to the Jew, then to the Gentile.

Romans 1:16

L ORD,
    How can we ever thank you for your salvation? You have chosen us, rescued us from the darkness of this world, and given us a future and a hope with you forever. You have "blessed us in the heavenly realms with every spiritual blessing in Christ," and we have everything we need to live a life of faith in you each day (Eph. 1:3).

I pray that my son's salvation would set him apart as your child. Give him your power and equip him to bless others and make the world a brighter place. May his kindness, generosity, wisdom, and self-control be remarkable as a sign that he is yours. Use your light in him to reveal yourself to those who need you desperately.

Enable my son to commit to following you. Give him knowledge and understanding of your Word so he can clearly express the message of your gospel. Ground his faith in truth and wisdom, rather than emotional experiences that come and go. May his hope and joy in knowing you be too wonderful to keep to himself. Use my son to lead others to Jesus.

Give my son compassion for the lost. Prompt him to pray for friends and family members who don't know you as their Savior. Give him courage to declare his allegiance to you and your Word.

Let my son be a light that shines before men, bringing praise to your glorious name.

Your gift of salvation is too amazing to keep a secret. May we speak of your goodness and all you have done to everyone who will listen. Keep us faithful and full of hope until we see you face-to-face. Amen.

A Prayer Story

The first indication that something was wrong was the low moaning I heard from the other room. I wiped my hands on the dish towel and walked briskly into the living room. My second son was curled up in a ball on the couch, holding his head. At age two, he couldn't tell me what was going on, but he kept repeating, "My head hurts," and "Tummy." Something was clearly wrong.

Quinn is my firecracker. Passionate, focused, empathetic to a fault, he has two speeds: full speed and asleep. So when he sat writhing in pain and clenching his hair I knew he was seriously sick. And my heart dropped with an immediate suspicion.

Within fifteen minutes, he began to throw up. I begged God that he would fall asleep and nap off the pain. In my heart, I knew what was happening but I was so full of dread for him that I couldn't speak it.

Over the next months this same pattern of pain would repeat itself on a fairly regular basis. I began to chart what was happening to him and talk to his doctors. Knowing how rare migraines are in very young children, I was thorough in my part to monitor him, watch for triggers, adjust his diet, and gather information so that we could get a diagnosis.

Thankfully, the doctors believed me and agreed with me. It seemed like Quinn was indeed suffering from debilitating migraines.

The process was grueling for us—waiting months for approvals for specialists, then insurance changes that meant starting the process all over again and convincing more doctors, and then waiting for specialists, and tests, and procedures. I was filled with gratitude when we took him for his first appointment with a pediatric neurologist. He officially diagnosed Quinn with migraines and then ordered a CAT scan. More months of waiting for approval, and more terrible headaches for my son, followed.

As much as taking my little boy to the children's hospital for a CAT scan made my heart churn, I was thrilled that we would finally get a good look inside and make sure his brain was normal. The day grew long, and the amazing nurses and staff at the hospital took us to the room to prep Quinn for anesthesia. I held my little boy in my arms as he trembled in fear and carried his body into the CAT scan room, careful not to trip over the cords that led to the various parts of machinery that would be attached to him. I held his hands and kissed his head as I laid him on the table and tried to be brave when the anesthesia coursed into his body, burning him for a moment before he cried out and then fell asleep. And then I somehow walked away from his limp body to wait.

The waiting room was filled with parents whose children practically lived at this hospital. Major issues of illnesses I couldn't even imagine were the norm for these families. And although I was brokenhearted for my own son, I couldn't help but be so grateful for the good health we did enjoy. God was giving me a good dose of perspective.

A couple weeks later, we met with his pediatric neurologist. He had bad news and good news. The good news was that his brain looked perfectly normal—no tumors!

The bad news was that he had major sinus disease and ear disease. The doctor could see five separate fluid-filled pockets in his sinuses alone! His neurologist explained that this could be causing Quinn's migraines. I was thrilled and sad all at the same time. Quinn never complained that his ears hurt, and although he had a runny nose most of the time, we thought it was related to a previous allergy diagnosis.

Several more specialists, courses of medication, natural therapy, and lots of prayer later, and we are still simply trying to manage Quinn's migraines.

What all of this boils down to for me, as a mother who loves her children and wants the best for them, is this:

God loves Quinn more than I do. God knows the number of hairs on Quinn's head and I don't. God planned all of Quinn's days before the foundation of the world. God wove Quinn together, sinuses and ear canals too, in my womb to be this exact child. God has a good plan for Quinn. God is not surprised by what is happening. God makes no mistakes in Quinn's life. God will use this in the lives of his siblings to shape them to be more Christlike too.

When I found out I was pregnant, I prayed that God would never allow my kids to suffer from migraines. As a migraine sufferer myself, I knew that it was genetic in our family. And yet God allowed that to be a part of my son's life at a young age. I could have been very bitter toward God, but through prayer and reading my Bible, I am able to hand over my son's health issues to the Lord and trust that this will in some way be used in Quinn's life to make him more like Christ.

My little boy's first response when a migraine hits is to ask me to pray. He breathes heavily, twisting and turning in pain, and holds my hand as Mommy lifts him up to God. He trembles as he prays for relief, but he trusts that God will bring it.

One thing I know—that when we are weak, we are strong. Relying on God's strength and grace, even at age two or three, is never a bad thing. As his mother, I don't want Quinn to suffer. But in my heart, I know that God allows the suffering in this fallen world to honor him. And I see how this trial is already shaping the heart of my son. I couldn't ask for anything more for my children.

Instead of trying to eradicate all this suffering from their lives, I know that this is a teaching time for all of us in our family to learn to accept our trials, put our trust in God to bring good from this hard situation, and to look beyond our present suffering to a better future with Christ.

This world will present us with pain. It will offer brokenness. It will foster suffering. But it doesn't define us. We are not our brokenness. We are more than conquerors. And although I didn't want my son to learn this lesson at age three, it's a beautiful thing to see him strong, prayerful, and trusting his Savior. God trumped my prayer for perfect health by answering my biggest prayer of all for my sons—that God would do whatever it takes to shape them to be like Christ, and if migraines are the vehicle to do it, then let it be.

A budding novelist, **Amber Lia** is a mother of three young boys and writes about faith and family at www.motherofknights.com. She and her husband, Guy, started a faith-friendly and family-friendly production company, Storehouse Media Group, with the goal of producing TV and feature films in Hollywood that honor God and inspire others.

46

When He's One of a Kind

For you created my inmost being; you knit me together in my mother's womb. I praise you because I am fearfully and wonderfully made; your works are wonderful, I know that full well. My frame was not hidden from you when I was made in the secret place, when I was woven together in the depths of the earth. Your eyes saw my unformed body; all the days ordained for me were written in your book before one of them came to be.

Psalm 139:13–16

Train up a child in the way he should go; even when he is old he will not depart from it.

Proverbs 22:6 ESV

You have searched me, LORD, and you know me. You know when I sit and when I rise; you perceive my thoughts from afar. You discern my going out and my lying down; you are familiar with all my ways.

Psalm 139:1–3

L ORD,
I thank you for creating my son. You planned and know every detail of his personality, talents, and dreams. You put the beautiful color in his eyes and the curve of a smile on his face. You know what makes him laugh, the heroes he admires, and the great things he dreams of accomplishing someday. You know him through and through and love him completely.

My son feels pulled between his desire to stand out as unique and the pressure to conform and fit in with everyone else. He can lose his confidence that he's a special individual, set apart by you as his child. He may copy the language, interests, and attitudes of the boys around him to feel like he belongs. Help him to see that he's yours—created, accepted, and loved—so he's free to discover who he truly is.

I pray for your insight into understanding the unique qualities of my child. Give me discernment to know what motivates him. What skills and abilities I should encourage and support. How to express love in a way he can really feel. When he needs space and when I should press in closer. How to share about you in ways that will capture his heart and mind.

Give me a fresh appreciation for his individuality. Help me to value the parts of his personality that differ from mine. Keep me from pushing him to be the center of attention if he prefers to be quiet. Let me enjoy his lively personality if he's the life of the party. If his interests or hobbies are outside of my experience, let me give him all the support that I can. Guard me from pressuring him to become someone he's not—he's made in your image, not mine, and you are the author of his life.

Help me to release my son to live for you and not for me. May he discover your perfect will for his life, and may I give him full freedom to follow after you. He truly is "fearfully and wonderfully made," and I praise your name for allowing me to be his parent. Amen.

47

When He's Holding a Grudge

Get rid of all bitterness, rage and anger, brawling and slander, along with every form of malice. Be kind and compassionate to one another, forgiving each other, just as in Christ God forgave you.

Ephesians 4:31–32

Don't have anything to do with foolish and stupid arguments, because you know they produce quarrels. And the Lord's servant must not be quarrelsome but must be kind to everyone, able to teach, not resentful.

2 Timothy 2:23–24

See to it that no one falls short of the grace of God and that no bitter root grows up to cause trouble and defile many.

Hebrews 12:15

Therefore, as God's chosen people, holy and dearly loved, clothe yourselves with compassion, kindness, humility, gentleness and patience.

Bear with each other and forgive one another if any of you has a grievance against someone. Forgive as the Lord forgave you.

Colossians 3:12–13

F ATHER,
     You are a God of justice, peace, and forgiveness. Thank you for keeping every one of your promises and giving your faithful love that never ends. Thank you for always speaking the truth so we can trust you in every way.

You know our pain of living in this broken world where we don't receive the same considerate, fair treatment from everyone around us. We are insulted, disregarded, abused, and cheated in countless ways. In our weakness we find ourselves guilty of the very things we resent in others.

My son is struggling with a hard heart against someone who offended him. It's difficult for him to forgive when he feels he was treated so unfairly. The relationship is broken and trust is gone. Whether he'll admit it or not, he'd like to take revenge and see the person "get what's coming to them."

This resentment is growing into bitterness in my son's heart. It's stealing his joy and creating distance from you and others. He's focusing so much on his own hurt and anger that he's forgotten how loved he is. He's pointing his finger at the other person's mistakes and ignoring how much grace and forgiveness he's received himself. This "bitter root" is creating trouble for my son and he needs your help.

Give my son the strength to release his anger and pain to you. Soften his heart so he can forgive. Give him patience to bear with their weaknesses and failings, and give him gratitude for the patience and mercy he's been given. Give him wisdom as he speaks, guarding him from slandering others and stirring up conflict.

Set my son free from this grudge that is tearing his spirit apart. Restore him to you and bring unity to this divided relationship. Reveal your power, grace, and kindness to my son, and may he become like Christ as he gives compassion to others.

Thank you for loving us in our weakness. You give us new minds and hearts to be light in this dark world. I praise you for the peace you offer in every situation. Amen.

48

When He's Dreaming about the Future

Take delight in the LORD, and he will give you the desires of your heart. Commit your way to the LORD; trust in him and he will do this: He will make your righteous reward shine like the dawn, your vindication like the noonday sun.

Psalm 37:4–6

Commit to the LORD whatever you do, and he will establish your plans. . . . In their hearts humans plan their course, but the LORD establishes their steps.

Proverbs 16:3, 9

Trust in the LORD with all your heart and lean not on your own understanding; in all your ways submit to him, and he will make your paths straight.

Proverbs 3:5–6

FATHER,
        I thank you today for the future you've planned for my son. Even now you're preparing him for what's in store as he grows in knowledge and wisdom. You're using every challenge and experience to stretch and shape him into the man you created him to be. I praise

you for coming into this world so my son would "have life, and have it to the full" (John 10:10). In you, his future is bright and full of hope.

Turn my son's heart toward you and your will. Let him joyfully discover your perfect plans for his education, career, relationships, and service to your church. May he long to follow you in every decision and opportunity that comes his way.

Rescue my son from the lies of this world. He will be pressured to pursue selfish ambition and success. He'll be told his worth lies in popularity and performance. Let him find his true peace and satisfaction in living out your path for his life.

Help my son to trust you when barriers to his dreams and goals arise. Give him peace that you're in control, and that you'll clear the way for him to go exactly where you want him to be. May he make decisions prayerfully and by your Word, being led by your Spirit rather than his own understanding. Give him patience to see your will accomplished in his life.

Give my son faith and trust in you. May he submit himself to you in every aspect of his life. Be glorified as he lives out your purposes day by day. Amen.

49

When He Needs His Parents' Influence

Listen, my son, to your father's instruction and do not forsake your mother's teaching. They are a garland to grace your head and a chain to adorn your neck. . . . Listen to your father, who gave you life, and do not despise your mother when she is old.

Proverbs 1:8–9; 23:22

Listen, my son, accept what I say, and the years of your life will be many. I instruct you in the way of wisdom and lead you along straight paths. When you walk, your steps will not be hampered; when you run, you will not stumble. Hold on to instruction, do not let it go; guard it well, for it is your life.

Proverbs 4:10–13

FATHER,
        As my son grows older and craves independence, he seems to tune out my voice more and more. He becomes impatient when I ask about his day or check on his homework and chores. He'd rather spend time with friends, online, or playing video games than spend time with me. I'm afraid I'm losing his heart as he resists my influence in his life.

My son will have difficult questions and decisions to navigate as he grows. He needs the benefits of my knowledge and experience as he makes his way in this world. Guard our relationship from any division that could silence my voice in his life. Build trust and security between us so he keeps an open ear to what I have to say. Humble his heart to realize he's not ready to face the challenges of life alone—he needs his loving heavenly Father and his parents to lead and help him along his way.

Give me wisdom to know how to guide and teach him. Show me when he needs comfort and a listening ear, and when he needs my instruction and authority. Help me know when to step back and allow him to test his independence. Make me a strong source of encouragement with every new challenge and adventure he may face.

Most of all, show me how to point my son to you. Let every word of counsel, every rule and boundary, and every effort to guide him be patterned after your truth. Make me prayerful for his future and full of praise for what you're doing in his life. Use me to reveal your love and wisdom. Keep us close and help us to walk with you together. Amen.

50

When I Give Him Too Much

Keep falsehood and lies far from me; give me neither poverty nor riches, but give me only my daily bread. Otherwise, I may have too much and disown you and say, "Who is the LORD?" Or I may become poor and steal, and so dishonor the name of my God.

Proverbs 30:8–9

Do not be afraid, little flock, for your Father has been pleased to give you the kingdom. Sell your possessions and give to the poor. Provide purses for yourselves that will not wear out, a treasure in heaven that will never fail, where no thief comes near and no moth destroys. For where your treasure is, there your heart will be also.

Luke 12:32–34

FATHER,
    Thank you for pouring blessings into my son's life. He has never wanted for food, clothing, shelter, fun, education, or love and affection. He's been sheltered and nurtured. Read to and played with. Coached and taught. Socialized and entertained. He has a wonderful life surrounded by love and good things.

My efforts to show love and generosity to my son have begun to foster a sense of entitlement. Instead of saying "Thank you," he's now saying, "What's next?" His expectations for birthday and Christmas gifts are growing out-of-bounds. He complains about not having the latest devices and expensive vacations like his classmates. He's easily bored, careless with his belongings, and running out of room to keep his things organized. I'm afraid that instead of blessing him, I've spoiled him in the end.

Help my son to love people more than possessions. Let him value his character more than his belongings. May he pursue what will last for eternity—generosity, justice, compassion, and love for others. Give him a heart that loves you more than anything, and let him recognize you as the source of all he has. Restore a grateful heart to my son so he can discover joy in what truly matters most.

Give me wisdom to show restraint when I'm shopping. Keep me from giving him instant gratification so he learns patience. Teach me how to stay firm when he won't take no for an answer. Create opportunities for us to bless others together and share what we have. Let us be defined by our love, not our possessions.

I pray that both my son and I would take your Word to heart:

> But godliness with contentment is great gain. For we brought nothing into the world, and we can take nothing out of it. But if we have food and clothing, we will be content with that. Those who want to get rich fall into temptation and a trap and into many foolish and harmful desires that plunge people into ruin and destruction. For the love of money is a root of all kinds of evil. Some people, eager for money, have wandered from the faith and pierced themselves with many griefs. (1 Tim. 6:6–10)

Spare us the grief that comes from loving your gifts more than we love you. Show me when the best gift for him is to buy no gift at all. Guard my son from any kind of greed. Bless him with contentment and godliness all the days of his life. Amen.

His Purity

God did not call us to be impure, but to live a holy life.

1 Thessalonians 4:7

Among you there must not be even a hint of sexual immorality, or of any kind of impurity, or of greed, because these are improper for God's holy people.

Ephesians 5:3

Sex is a wonderful servant but a horrific master.

Augustine[4]

We live today in a sexually charged society. This reality manifests itself in unique ways for our sons and daughters. Our daughters are taught to use sex to find relationships, and our sons are taught to use relationships to get sex. Where the rites of passage to adulthood used to be areas of character, independence, and responsibility, kids are now defining their "maturity" by watching R-rated movies, listening to sexually explicit music, or playing video games with an "M" rating. Sexual activity has become a symbol of manhood for our culture.

With fewer and fewer men remaining in the home to guide their boys to adulthood, young men are lost and must resort to letting society tell them what a real man is. The other reality is that everywhere our boys look they are inundated with sexual images and language. The culture lies to our kids that "everyone is doing it." Even boys with the most supportive parents, excellent role models, and best intentions still have to fight the lust of the flesh that is staring them in the face everywhere they turn. It's a challenge to convince kids that the reason God has told them to abstain from sex until marriage is because of his love for them.

While our boys are hearing so many messages encouraging them to become sexually active as early as possible, there isn't a strong opposing voice speaking about the physical, mental, and emotional consequences of sex outside of marriage. Why should they believe there is a better and more excellent way? How do we persuade them that God's plan is in their best interest? When movies, television shows, and song lyrics assume that sex is a part of every dating relationship, what will encourage them to save themselves for their wife? By being offered the freedom to share intimacy with anyone and everyone, our sons are unaware of the truth that through sex "the two will become one flesh" (1 Cor. 6:16).

It breaks my heart to see the way casual sex has brought pain, confusion, and physical harm to our young people. They suffer high rates of disease, teen pregnancy, abortion, and emotional turmoil because they don't understand the risks and consequences of their actions. We can see why God has set such a high standard of purity for the children he loves.

Addiction to pornography by both men and women is at an all-time high. It continues to grow, permanently distorting the beauty of intimacy in marriage. It's no longer a secret activity in front of a computer or television in the basement—porn can be accessed on phones and tablets, letting boys essentially carry it in their back pocket at all times. It's scary as a parent to hear that the average age a boy first views pornography is only eight years old.[5] This is an area that parents can pray specifically for their sons' protection, as it can have a permanent impact on their relationship with God and their marriage.

Pray that the Lord will establish your son's footsteps in his Word. Pray that sexual sin will never trap him in addiction. Pray for wisdom to know how to protect his innocence. This might mean setting up internet filters on your computer, limiting internet access to the public places in your home, and staying mindful of the entertainment choices he's making. Seek godly counsel on when and how it's appropriate to talk to your kids about sex, dating, and the dangers of pornography. Ask the Lord to equip you to teach your son what healthy, godly sexuality and relationships look like. And pray that if he does stumble, that God would bring him to repentance and draw your son closer to himself.

Many of us have compromised our sexual purity in the past in ways we deeply regret. Parents can feel they've disqualified themselves from holding their sons to God's standard since they've failed in that area themselves. We're afraid of being hypocrites by asking them to live out values we didn't hold to ourselves. It's important to remember that in Christ, we are new creations. The person you are today *does* know the truth and seeks to live by it. Don't let the enemy's lies keep you from encouraging your son to stay pure because of your own sins. The Lord has already forgiven and removed them "as far as the east is from the west" (Ps. 103:12).

While I don't think it's wise to burden our kids with every detail of our past mistakes, we can use them to help our sons understand that sexual sin and temptation are universal struggles for every person. They'll be encouraged by having a parent who can show compassion for what they're going through. The Lord himself can identify with what our sons experience.

> We do not have a high priest who is unable to empathize with our weaknesses, but we have one who has been tempted in every way, just as we are—yet he did not sin. Let us then approach God's throne of grace with confidence, so that we may receive mercy and find grace to help us in our time of need. (Heb. 4:15–16)

Because of Christ, our sons don't have to handle temptation alone. We can encourage our sons to make mindful choices along the way, not giving ground in small areas that will lead to giving up everything in the end. We can support him in seeking friends and mentors who follow the Lord and give accountability if his commitment to purity is shaken. We can set boundaries around his social activities and entertainment choices that could influence his attitudes toward women and sex. And we can pray that he'll trust God for his future—that God intends for him to have an incredible, loving relationship with his bride that's satisfying in every way.

When we see so many young people rejecting the values they were raised with, we can wonder if praying really does any good. We can think "boys will be boys," and give up believing our influence and prayers make a difference. Don't give up hope and lay aside the spiritual power of prayer for your child. God promises in his Word that "this is the confidence we have in approaching God: that if we ask anything according to his will, he hears us. And if we know that he hears us—whatever we ask—we know that we have what we asked of him" (1 John 5:14–15). Ask him to strengthen your faith as you place your son in his hands.

For parents who are grieving because their sons compromised their purity and innocence in some way, take heart. God is in the business of making us new. He offers forgiveness, restoration, and a new beginning. Ask for his help in working through your anger and disappointment. Ask him to restore the trust that's been lost between you. Guard your mind from self-blame and the "what ifs" we burden ourselves with as parents. Share Scriptures with your son about God's grace, such as 1 John 1:9, "If we confess our sins, he is faithful and just and will forgive us our sins and purify us from all unrighteousness."

Our Father treasures our sons in every way, just as we do. In him we find hope for our sons' futures and who they'll become. In the Lord our boys can find the strength they need to follow him in every area of life. Let's never give up encouraging our sons and covering them in prayer.

51

When He Considers Dating

Above all else, guard your heart, for everything you do flows from it.

Proverbs 4:23

Flee the evil desires of youth and pursue righteousness, faith, love and peace, along with those who call on the Lord out of a pure heart.

2 Timothy 2:22

Love must be sincere. Hate what is evil; cling to what is good. Be devoted to one another in love. Honor one another above yourselves. Never be lacking in zeal, but keep your spiritual fervor, serving the Lord.

Romans 12:9–11

And this is my prayer: that your love may abound more and more in knowledge and depth of insight, so that you may be able to discern what is best and may be pure and blameless for the day of Christ.

Philippians 1:9–10

FATHER,
   In your perfect wisdom you created romance, marriage, and families. Even now you're preparing my son's heart to love and commit to his bride. On his road toward marriage he may relate with young women who will shape the man and husband he'll become. He needs your help to guard his heart and make wise decisions about every relationship.

   Give my son a desire to honor and protect the girls in his life. Let him cherish each young lady not just as a friend or romantic attachment, but as a priceless creation of God. May he devote himself to praying for and serving the young women you place around him.

Let his words be respectful and kind, full of encouragement and affirmation of the unique qualities they possess. Use him to share his knowledge of you and your selfless love with every girl he meets. Our culture will encourage him to use young women as objects for his own gratification. Guard him from dating simply to boost his self-image and reputation. Give him eyes to see past a girl's appearance to her heart, so he can value her inner beauty. Give him a passion for what is good and pure so he'll run from any sexual temptation that dating can bring.

Give my son discernment to date for the right reasons. May he guard his heart so he doesn't squander his attention and affection on just any girl who makes herself available. Keep him from dating simply for fun—keep his mind fixed on preparing for the marriage you have in store. Help him to honor and respect my counsel as he makes decisions about dating relationships.

Let me set an example of a believer living sincerely for you. May I have a gentle, gracious spirit that my son will want to both imitate and find in his loved one. Prepare me even now to embrace the girl who captures my son's heart. Help me to encourage them in their obedience and love for you. Teach me to trust you with his future instead of trying to control every dating decision he makes. Your will is good and perfect—I pray he will discover your wonderful plan as he looks for love.

Thank you for my son and all the wonderful qualities he shares with his friends and loved ones. Draw him near to you as he shares his heart with others. Amen.

52

When He Can Be a Leader

Don't let anyone look down on you because you are young, but set an example for the believers in speech, in conduct, in love, in faith and in purity.

1 Timothy 4:12

Jesus called them together and said, "You know that the rulers of the Gentiles lord it over them, and their high officials exercise authority over them. Not so with you. Instead, whoever wants to become great among you must be your servant, and whoever wants to be first must be your slave—just as the Son of Man did not come to be served, but to serve, and to give his life as a ransom for many."

Matthew 20:25–28

Since an overseer manages God's household, he must be blameless— not overbearing, not quick-tempered, not given to drunkenness, not violent, not pursuing dishonest gain. Rather, he must be hospitable, one who loves what is good, who is self-controlled, upright, holy and disciplined. He must hold firmly to the trustworthy message as it has been taught, so that he can encourage others by sound doctrine and refute those who oppose it.

Titus 1:7–9

L ORD,
I pray that you would equip my son to serve as a leader. Even now, I pray he would be one who "loves what is good, who is self-controlled, upright, holy and disciplined." Allow him to hold fast to the truth of your Word, and enable him to teach its message to everyone. As his future unfolds, use my son to lead his classmates, coworkers, and family to a deeper knowledge of you.

Give my son a heart that loves to serve. Show him how to use his strengths and talents to care and help. Fill him with confidence that his efforts can make a difference in this dark world. Let him reveal the love of Christ as he works to lead, teach, and give of himself to others.

Prepare my son even now to lead his family in love and godliness. Provide opportunities for him to take on unique responsibilities at school. Bring him respect and influence in his workplace, equipping him to perform his job with integrity. Use his energy, commitment, and respect for authority as an example to any team or organization he's part of. Enable my son to be a leader by living according to your perfect standards alone.

Guard my son's speech from lies, profanity, complaining, or insults that will compromise his credibility. Let him control his temper and show self-control. Give him humility so he doesn't become pushy or abusive to others. Protect him from any addiction to drugs, alcohol, pornography, or gambling that could take over his life. Make him disciplined to do his work thoroughly and gain a reputation for faithfulness and reliability. Build him up as an example to others by displaying your goodness and holiness in his life.

Thank you for being our perfect leader. All your ways are perfect and you love us completely. We can trust you to take us exactly where we should go, and to teach us how to live and know you. Give us hearts that submit to your authority in every way. Help us to follow you every day of our lives. Amen.

53

When He's Feeling Depressed

I will glory in the LORD; let the afflicted hear and rejoice. . . . I sought
the LORD, and he answered me; he delivered me from all my fears. . . .
The LORD is close to the brokenhearted and saves those who are
crushed in spirit.

Psalm 34:2, 4, 18

My soul is weary with sorrow; strengthen me according to your word.

Psalm 119:28

A cheerful heart is good medicine, but a crushed spirit dries up the
bones.

Proverbs 17:22

O LORD my God, I cried to you for help, and you have healed me. . . .
You have turned for me my mourning into dancing; you have loosed
my sackcloth and clothed me with gladness, that my glory may sing
your praise and not be silent. O LORD my God, I will give thanks to
you forever!

Psalm 30:2, 11–12 ESV

FATHER,
     You know the pain, disappointment, and sorrow we experi-
ence in this life. You know how it feels to be alone and betrayed. We
suffer illness and injury, failure and embarrassment, and the loss of
dreams and loved ones. In your kindness you bring us comfort and
the strength to keep on going.

My son is hurting and has lost his joy. The friendships and activities he usually enjoys have lost their appeal. His energy is low; he's
unmotivated to pursue his goals or what he needs to accomplish each

day. I miss his laughter and enthusiasm. I'm afraid he won't be able to overcome the negativity that's taken over his spirit. Only you can rescue him from depression and despair.

Bring your perfect healing to my son's heart. Guard his mind from dwelling on his pain. Help him to see through the lie that today's troubles will last forever. Let him remember your love—may he trust in your power to save him and care for his every need.

Replace my son's worrying and complaining with gratitude and peace. Surround him with family and friends who love him deeply to protect him from isolation. Give him strength and endurance to walk through this valley without giving up hope.

Show me how to build up my son. Give me wisdom to know how to encourage him. Direct me in providing any medical or spiritual support that will help in his healing. Guard my heart from fear and worry—let me trust you fully to restore my son's peace and joy.

Thank you for turning our "mourning into dancing." You are near, you are strong, and your love is beyond what we can imagine. Amen.

54

When He Needs a Good Friend

Do not be yoked together with unbelievers. For what do righteousness and wickedness have in common? Or what fellowship can light have with darkness?

2 Corinthians 6:14

The righteous choose their friends carefully, but the way of the wicked leads them astray.

Proverbs 12:26

Two are better than one, because they have a good return for their
labor: If either of them falls down, one can help the other up. But
pity anyone who falls and has no one to help them up. Also, if two
lie down together, they will keep warm. But how can one keep warm
alone? Though one may be overpowered, two can defend themselves.
A cord of three strands is not quickly broken.

Ecclesiastes 4:9–12

L ORD,
       Thank you for the gift of friendship. You know how an encour-
aging word, shared laughter with others, and a sense of belonging
add joy to our lives. Our friends can bring out the best in us and give
us memories for a lifetime. When we suffer through challenges and
loss, our friends give comfort and help when we need them most. We
feel your love through the kindness of those you've placed around us.

I pray that my son would find a strong, loyal friend of his own.
Bring someone into his life who accepts him as he is and makes him
feel valued. Help him find more than a playmate—a friend who builds
him up, cheers him on to pursue his goals, and encourages him to
follow you. Create a relationship that stands firm through challenges
and disagreements. May his friend be not just a companion but a
spiritual brother in Christ. Join with them to create a "cord of three
strands" that lasts through time.

Give my son discernment to reach out to those who will treat him
with respect and kindness. Don't let him settle for relationships that
will tear him down just to avoid feeling alone. Give him patience to
wait for the best friendships you have in store.

Prepare my son even now to be a gift to others. Teach him generosity and thoughtfulness. Let him learn to put others first and listen to
what they have to say. Give him a compassionate heart that's eager
to help and encourage those around him. Make him your light and
reveal yourself through his love and obedience.

Thank you that, through Jesus, we are called the friends of God.
Reveal to my son how close you are to him—you listen, you care,

you give your strength, and you share in every sorrow and joy he will experience. In you he is never alone. Amen.

55

When He Needs a Good Example

As iron sharpens iron, so one person sharpens another.

Proverbs 27:17

And let us consider how we may spur one another on toward love and good deeds, not giving up meeting together, as some are in the habit of doing, but encouraging one another—and all the more as you see the Day approaching.

Hebrews 10:24–25

Teach the older men to be temperate, worthy of respect, self-controlled, and sound in faith, in love and in endurance. . . . Similarly, encourage the young men to be self-controlled. In everything set them an example by doing what is good.

Titus 2:2, 6–7

FATHER,
Growing up in this world can be difficult and confusing. My son faces temptations to live for himself and turn away from your truth. He can become discouraged by failure at school or rejection by other kids. His interests fluctuate and he's not sure he'll ever find his true talents or dreams. The athletes and celebrities he admires experience failure and shame, and he wonders if there are any heroes

to be found. The challenges he'll face as he journeys toward adulthood seem overwhelming.

In your great mercy you understand that he needs help to find his way. You gave your Word, your Spirit, and our family to build him up in every situation. I pray you would also surround my son with godly men to encourage him and teach him how to follow you.

My son needs the gift of a mentor to come alongside him right now. He needs to see a man's faith lived out in hard times. Let him see an example of generosity to the needy. Self-control in the face of temptation. Endurance when there's difficult work to be done. Patience and forgiveness for the weak and immature. A helping hand to those who are struggling. Faithful friendship that sticks close no matter what. Knowledge of your Word and persistence in prayer. He needs to see *you* in the lives of men around him.

Place a burden for my son on the hearts of mature men of faith, so they'll draw near and care for him. Create opportunities for them to connect. Open my son's heart to welcome their influence. Give him ears to hear their teaching and advice. Speak through the words of his mentors so he can discover your truth and your will.

Thank you that my son doesn't have to figure out life on his own. I praise you for loving us through other believers. I trust you will equip my son to become a spiritual leader himself someday. Train him and use him for Christ's sake. Amen.

56

When He Needs to Wait

Do not be anxious about anything, but in every situation, by prayer and petition, with thanksgiving, present your requests to God. And the peace of God, which transcends all understanding, will guard your hearts and your minds in Christ Jesus.

Philippians 4:6–7

Hope deferred makes the heart sick, but a longing fulfilled is a tree of life.

Proverbs 13:12

Those who hope in the LORD will renew their strength. They will soar on wings like eagles; they will run and not grow weary, they will walk and not be faint.

Isaiah 40:31

I remain confident of this: I will see the goodness of the LORD in the land of the living. Wait for the LORD; be strong and take heart and wait for the LORD.

Psalm 27:13–14

FATHER,
    Thank you for your good and perfect plans for my son's life. He has so much to look forward to and wonderful hopes for the future. It's difficult, however, to wait for what's in store.

I pray you will teach my son patience and faith in every situation that comes his way. He'll have to wait for his grade report after a challenging semester. He'll wonder if he's accepted by his favorite school and what kind of financial aid he'll receive. Job opportunities, romantic interests, team tryouts, auditions, trips, and summer camps—all these possibilities can take time to develop and come to pass. He becomes frustrated with wondering and waiting to know what will happen.

My son will also need endurance to make it through tough times. An injury can require lengthy rest for healing. A difficult class can demand hours of extra study and stress. Strained friendships take time and persistence to mend. It may take many weeks of allowance and extra jobs to save up for something important. Give my son your strength and help to wait for your answers to prayer.

Help my son to live in the moment instead of dwelling on what's to come. Focus his energy on the relationships and responsibilities of today so he can give them his full attention. Make him grateful for the blessings of each day without becoming lost in wishful thinking. Give him a tenacious spirit to keep working toward his goals without giving up.

Teach him to trust you—let him learn to pray continually and find your peace. Use times of waiting and wondering to turn his heart toward you. Make him eager to discover your will for every area of his life. Let him surrender his hopes and dreams to your control, believing your timing and plans are perfect. Give him peace and patience as he places all things in your hands.

Thank you for not giving us everything we want, when we want it. In your goodness you teach us to wait for you. You give us rest when we're worried and impatient. You satisfy our deepest longings and give us hope for tomorrow. You are everything we need. Amen.

A Prayer Story

We do not know what we ought to pray for, but the Spirit himself intercedes for us through wordless groans.

Romans 8:26

Our oldest son was six when we met him, seven when he came to live with us, and eight when he legally became ours. We knew his early years of trauma and neglect would pose challenges as he struggled to fit into a healthy parent-child relationship. He longed to control us. He longed to control every little detail of his life, and yet much of the time he presented himself as the perfect child. After the initial year of settling into our family, we only rarely saw the rage he kept beneath the surface; every four to six months it would rear its ugly head for a week or two, and we would emerge physically bruised and emotionally battered. As quickly as it had begun, the storm would pass, and he would once again become "perfect."

It would be several years before we discovered just how much fear and fury our son held within his heart. We moved our growing family into a much-needed bigger home in May 2012, when he was twelve and a half. While we anticipated a bit of emotional backlash from our son, who suffers from reactive attachment disorder and was also showing the first signs of adolescence, we had no idea the devastating effect this would have on him. The five and a half years spent living in our little one-bathroom ranch had been the only stable years of his life, and the upheaval of moving was too much for him to handle. His calm façade crumbled.

When your parent-heart is breaking and your worst fears are being realized, you begin to pray in a completely foreign way. Gone were my nightly mutterings of "God, please help him grow into a responsible man of God." Those simple fair-weather prayers were replaced by gut-wrenching, sobbing pleas as my son slipped further and further away. He was uncontrollable. Daily fits of violent rage gave way to a series of stays in a mental health facility, several 911 calls, trips to the emergency room, threats on the lives of my husband, myself, and our unborn baby, and ultimately an arrest. My heart became numb. I was angry, exhausted, and spiritually unable to hold my head above water. I kept my little purple Bible with me always, and while I had little ability to read it or decipher it in those darkest of days, I slept with one hand clasping it beneath my pillow. The Spirit groaned within me as I cried out to God, and I knew he heard my every need.

For several months, as our traumatized son acted out within the walls of juvenile detention, my husband worked feverishly on his behalf, leaving no stone unturned in his quest to find help. We were directed and redirected, offered useless services, put off, and ignored. Everyone agreed it wasn't safe to bring him home, yet no one offered solutions. We wanted to find a facility that would help him, not just lock him away, but our insurance refused assistance, as did Medicaid, adoption subsidy, and every other state or federal entity we contacted. The advice given from more than one "authority" left us shocked; we were advised to abandon our son, to relinquish our rights as his parents because funds were more readily available for children who had been abandoned. We refused. God our Father has never given up on us in our rebellion, and we would not give up on our son. We continued to wait on the Lord, and he blessed us with his peace, along with the assurance that every door would be closed besides the one he had chosen.

At the last possible second, hours away from a hearing in which the courts would decide our son's future, our church offered to pay the entrance fees and first month's tuition for a therapeutic boarding school we had been in contact with, a Christian facility designed to help struggling young men. While all other doors had closed, these arrangements fell into line effortlessly: the court, the school, funding, the men who helped transport our son . . . every detail was perfectly orchestrated. We couldn't afford this school and had no idea how we would pay for the second month's tuition, yet we stepped out in faith knowing this was God's chosen path. A year and a half later, God has continued to supply each tuition payment.

Our son is doing remarkably well, and we've never doubted that he's where he needs to be. The school is full of godly men who genuinely care about him and his future, and we're seeing the evidence of maturity and self-control. My biggest prayer now is that God will hold my son when I cannot, and that he'll show us when it's time to bring him home.

....

Lisa is the happy wife of a hilarious bearded man and a home-schooling mom to six beautiful children, two of whom joined the family through older-child adoption. She writes about raising children with reactive attachment disorder, her crazy family, and her lifelong journey to overcome herself. Feel free to visit her at www .lisa-overcomingmyself.blogspot.com, but don't expect perfection; anything good in Lisa, she credits to Jesus. And hey! If you like to listen to starving musicians, you can check out their musical venture, The Growing Roots, at http://www.reverbnation.com/981069.

57

When He Needs His Parent

Be completely humble and gentle; be patient, bearing with one another in love. Make every effort to keep the unity of the Spirit through the bond of peace.

Ephesians 4:2–3

A father to the fatherless, a defender of widows, is God in his holy dwelling.

Psalm 68:5

Love is patient, love is kind. It does not envy, it does not boast, it is not proud. It does not dishonor others, it is not self-seeking, it is not easily angered, it keeps no record of wrongs. Love does not delight in evil but rejoices with the truth. It always protects, always trusts, always hopes, always perseveres. Love never fails.

1 Corinthians 13:4–8

LORD,
You are our perfect, faithful father. You take care of us when we bring our needs to you. Whenever we are lonely or afraid, we can run to you for comfort. You teach us what we need to know and share your

amazing wisdom for every confusing situation. You're our mighty protector when we're in danger. You share in every celebration and sorrow we experience. You're always close, patient, wise, and gentle.

There is no father on earth like you. Thank you for demonstrating the love of your father-heart through the care and kindness of our earthly parents. I pray that you would strengthen my son's relationship with me as his parent and reveal yourself to us in the midst of it.

Bring unity where there is division right now. Give us patience to hear each other's point of view. Keep us from a battle of wills, where our energy goes into winning instead of understanding one another. Give us forgiveness for any harsh, angry words that have been spoken. Humble us to admit where we're wrong and help us to begin again.

Give me the ability to accept him as he is. Help me to enjoy the unique qualities of my boy, whether we have much in common or not. Enable me to set my son free to follow the Lord's leading instead of trying to control his destiny.

Show us ways we can connect and enjoy time together. Make my son a high priority so he's not crowded out by work, entertainment, or hobbies. Give me the conviction that a quantity of time, not just quality, is needed to bind us together and give me lasting influence.

Draw us close to you. Let me discover the powerful truths in your Word so I can lead my son to Jesus. Help me to obey you in all things so I can set a strong example of integrity. Give me the fruit of the Spirit—love, joy, peace, patience, kindness, goodness, faithfulness, gentleness, and self-control—so my son can see the nature of God himself.

Thank you for being our Father. No matter how near or far, strong or weak our earthly parents may be, you're always with us and love us in every way. Let my son discover you as his true Father and walk with you every day of his life. Amen.

58

When He Has a Problem

And my God will meet all your needs according to the riches of his glory in Christ Jesus. To our God and Father be glory for ever and ever. Amen.

Philippians 4:19–20

So do not worry, saying, "What shall we eat?" or "What shall we drink?" or "What shall we wear?" For the pagans run after all these things, and your heavenly Father knows that you need them. But seek first his kingdom and his righteousness, and all these things will be given to you as well.

Matthew 6:31–33

The LORD is good, a refuge in times of trouble. He cares for those who trust in him.

Nahum 1:7

FATHER,
You know what my son needs today. He's been asking and waiting and wondering how this situation will work out. I don't have the means to provide for him myself. He's worried that time will run out before the solution comes through. He's anxious and afraid—he's not sure you hear him when he asks for help.

Thank you for giving my son a problem that he can't solve. You've backed him into a corner where you are his only hope. Use this time of need as a powerful means of revealing how good and faithful you are. You keep your promises and you care for us. Let him experience the riches of your glory and praise your name for coming to his rescue.

Give me faith to trust you to help my boy. When he's hungry, I feed him. When he's injured, I bandage his wounds. It's difficult to stand by this time, unable to free him from this difficulty. Quiet my heart to be still and wait in expectancy for the wonderful things you will do.

I pray that my son will seek your kingdom and righteousness above anything else. Give him a deep awareness of his spiritual need for you that's greater than any physical need he'll ever suffer. Let him love you now, even before you've brought relief. Teach him to pray and enable him to believe in you.

Help us to remember all you've done for us in the past. Give us grateful hearts for your kindness and generosity, rather than fretting and complaining about the problems of today. You are *always* faithful.

Thank you for loving my son. You are everything to us. You are our life. Amen.

59

When He Feels Pressure to Achieve

Am I now trying to win the approval of human beings, or of God? Or am I trying to please people? If I were still trying to please people, I would not be a servant of Christ.

Galatians 1:10

What do people get for all the toil and anxious striving with which they labor under the sun? All their days their work is grief and pain; even at night their minds do not rest. This too is meaningless. A person can do nothing better than to eat and drink and find satisfaction in their own toil. This too, I see, is from the hand of God.

Ecclesiastes 2:22–24

Whatever you do, work at it with all your heart, as working for the Lord, not for human masters, since you know that you will receive

an inheritance from the Lord as a reward. It is the Lord Christ you
are serving.

Colossians 3:23–24

FATHER,
It seems that my son is ranked and measured in every situation
he finds himself in. The kids all know who's at the top of the class, who
scored in the playoff game, who was voted class president, and who's
first chair in the band. They label each other according to popularity
and talent. My son bears the strain of wondering if he'll pass or fail, be
included or left out, or be named a winner or a loser. He can believe
that his worth as a person depends on his success.

Thank you for giving him your complete grace and acceptance. You
show compassion for his weakness and hold eternal rewards in your
hand. You offer peace and contentment—he doesn't have to strive
to earn your love and favor. You call him your friend and beloved
child no matter how he's graded by the world. In you he can find
peace just as he is.

Set my son free from the pressure to please other people. May he
love you with all his heart and seek to please *you* with his life. May he
work hard and use his gifts for your glory—not to impress others or
boost his self-image. Show him his worth in your eyes so he doesn't
depend on the praise of others to feel important.

Give my son a right perspective on his success and failures. If he
earns an excellent grade or reward, may he praise you for equipping
him to achieve. When he experiences failure or disappointment, let
him trust you to strengthen him and build him up. Help him to
see that every talent and ability comes from you to accomplish your
purposes in his life.

Give me wisdom in how I speak to my son. Show me how to encourage his efforts without pressuring him to live up to unreasonable
expectations. Help me to affirm his heart and character, not just his
test scores and trophies. Give me eyes to see his strengths and how
he's made in your image.

Thank you for the freedom we find in you. We can rest in your mercy and grace. You give us the hope of eternity with you. You promise to finish your work of making us perfect, like Christ. I praise you for your peace. Amen.

60

When He's Choosing Who to Worship

Those who cling to worthless idols turn away from God's love for them.

Jonah 2:8

Stand up and praise the LORD your God, who is from everlasting to everlasting. Blessed be your glorious name, and may it be exalted above all blessing and praise. You alone are the LORD. You made the heavens, even the highest heavens, and all their starry host, the earth and all that is on it, the seas and all that is in them. You give life to everything, and the multitudes of heaven worship you.

Nehemiah 9:5–6

Among the gods there is none like you, Lord; no deeds can compare with yours. All the nations you have made will come and worship before you, Lord; they will bring glory to your name. For you are great and do marvelous deeds; you alone are God. Teach me your way, LORD, that I may rely on your faithfulness; give me an undivided heart, that I may fear your name.

Psalm 86:8–11

LORD,
 In your Word you instruct us to worship you and you alone. Our hope for today and eternity lies in believing you are the one true God. You are perfect and holy, mighty and full of wisdom, and worthy of all our praise forever. When we discover you as our Lord and King, we find forgiveness, hope, and your presence for all time.

But it's so easy to forget the God we cannot see and place our hope in things on earth. The temptation to find our security and happiness in money, family, career success, or material possessions is strong. We can turn our friendships, physical health, and dreams into idols that we pursue at all costs. We put our hope in your gifts instead of the One who gives us everything we need.

I pray that my son would give you his heart. Give him a deep longing to know you and please you with his life. Let him acknowledge you as his Creator. Help him to trust that you're in control no matter how dark and broken this world can be. Open his mind to how great and magnificent you are—let him be awestruck by you!

My son will be tempted to give his heart's allegiance to friends and loved ones. He'll find work or education he's passionate about, and want to put all his energy into pursuing his goals. He may experience popularity or praise from others that holds more appeal than pleasing you. His first car, apartment, or girlfriend may become his pride and joy, replacing his satisfaction in you. Guard his heart so that nothing replaces the Lord in his life.

Make us faithful in our worship. Give us grateful hearts for all your goodness to us. Captivate us with your beautiful creation. Draw us to your church, praising you each week with those who love you. Keep your Word in our minds to keep us focused on your glory. Let us love you above all things until we see you face-to-face. Amen.

His Idols

Sing to the LORD a new song; sing to the LORD, all the earth. Sing to the LORD, praise his name; proclaim his salvation day after day. Declare his glory among the nations, his marvelous deeds among all peoples. For great is the LORD and most worthy of praise; he is to be feared above all gods. For all the gods of the nations are idols, but the LORD made the heavens. Splendor and majesty are before him; strength and glory are in his sanctuary.

Psalm 96:1–6

Every one of us is, even from his mother's womb, a master craftsman of idols.

John Calvin[6]

You don't have to go to heathen lands today to find false gods. America is full of them. Whatever you love more than God is your idol.

D. L. Moody[7]

When we hear the term *idol* we often picture an image made of wood, stone, or precious metals on a pedestal in a lofty temple. But idols have always had more to do with the heart than outward religious rituals. Every one of us will choose something or someone to attach our love, attention, and devotion to. That is why the Word tells us to "put to death, therefore, whatever belongs to your earthly nature: sexual immorality, impurity, lust, evil desires and greed, which is idolatry" (Col. 3:5). God knows when we're jealous, lustful, greedy, or losing our self-control, we're giving our hearts over to worship something in this world.

Our prayer for our sons is that they will find their satisfaction in God alone so they don't create idols in his place. Most of us are brought up to pursue the American Dream of a spouse, two kids, a nice house, and a dog. We spend years pursuing education and a successful career so we can "have it all." Advertisers know that sex sells, since we can believe the subtle lie that sexual appeal and fulfillment hold the key to happiness. We spend our lives searching for a sense of satisfaction, but that peace seems always out of reach. Until we discover that we'll only find true rest in the Lord, we'll keep on wrestling with disappointment and disillusionment.

It's hard to say what the idols of our sons' hearts may become. It's likely they will be linked to whatever gives them a sense of self-worth and success. If they fill their shelves with trophies and varsity letters, they may "bow down" to sports by spending every free moment training, competing, and watching ESPN. If they're constantly praised and rewarded for academic success, they could put their trust in diplomas and degrees. If they experience sexual gratification through pornography or the attention of women, they may pursue sex above all else. If image and social status have made them king of the hill, they could become workaholics to achieve wealth and material things. Their idols will be shaped around their own image, to satisfy their own desires and gain the approval of others.

Of course we'll be thankful if our sons achieve academic success, a comfortable living, and a beautiful family. The temptation lies in loving those gifts more than we love the giver—God. Our sons' talents, strengths, possessions, and relationships are part of the Lord's perfect plan for their lives. It's exciting to think about how they can use their resources to make the world a better place. We can pray they learn humility and gratitude to recognize that every good thing they have comes from God. We can pray that they hold everything with open hands and seek to discover how the Lord wants them to use what they've been given. And we can pray that they will love him with all of their heart, soul, and strength so nothing ever takes his place.

As parents, we can play a part in helping our sons to construct idols in their lives. In our attempts to encourage them to do their best, we can place a higher emphasis on their performance than their character. We can push them to "stand on their own two feet" instead of learning to depend on their heavenly Father who loves them. We can express anger and judgment when they fail, teaching a message that they have to earn our love (and God's as well) through their own perfection. We can focus on the goals of trophies and wealth rather than our sons' unique abilities to serve and give to others. We need to constantly pray for sensitive "radar" to identify our sons' true heart issues and needs so we don't inadvertently steer them away from God's truth and priorities.

God gave us an excellent picture of our heart's pull toward idolatry in the story of the Israelites in Exodus. One of the first temptations to build idols came when God didn't show up right when they wanted him to. Moses had traveled to a mountaintop to receive the Law from the Lord. As the Israelites waited at the bottom for his return, they grew impatient and started to doubt he was ever coming back. They assumed that God had forgotten them, so they pressured Aaron, their priest, to melt down their jewelry to make a golden calf to worship. I won't go into all the details, but let's just say this did not go over well when Moses finally came back down the mountain. If our son is waiting on God to meet a need or to answer prayer, and he doesn't receive a rapid response from the Lord that he's hoping for, his heart could turn away from God rather than trusting and waiting patiently.

Another stumbling block for the Israelites was the company they kept. God made it clear that he wanted his people to live differently, set apart from the nations surrounding them. Whenever the Israelites would intermarry or create alliances with their pagan neighbors, their hearts would fall away from devotion to their one true God. I can definitely see this pattern in my children's lives as well. When they immerse themselves in too much television, spending more time investing in their social lives than their families or church, and filling hour upon hour with online shopping and video games, their hearts lose a wholehearted desire to live for the Lord.

Finally, a significant barrier to our sons loving God with all their heart is resisting his authority. Sometimes God asks us to wait for what we want, whether it's a pay raise at work or saving sex for the marriage relationship. When God sets boundaries for our behavior or asks us to wait for a blessing, he's not trying to steal our joy and happiness. We can trust that everything he says and does is out of perfect love. As parents, we would never say yes to whatever our sons want, whenever they want it. Our homes would fall into chaos and we would be broke and exhausted!

If I gave my three-year-old son everything he wanted, he would ruin his teeth with candy and would play in the street with sharp objects. He doesn't always take no for an answer and will throw a tantrum to try to have his way. That pattern doesn't always leave us as we grow. It's difficult to swallow the word *no* whether we're three or seventy-three. We want to seek after our own desires and pleasures and reject any authority that stands in our way. Just as our kids can resist our advice, influence, and limits, we can reject our Lord and King out of a selfish, rebellious attitude.

Let's pray that our sons keep their desires, their hopes and dreams, and their blessings in proper perspective. We can ask that they seek God wholeheartedly and follow his leading in their life. Let us pray that they will hold on to faith that God is loving and good, even when he asks them to wait for whatever they're longing for. Let's pray that they will fill their minds with the truth of the Word rather than the popular philosophies and entertainment of the culture. Let us ask God to give them humble, submissive hearts to obey him in every way. When the Lord is the first love of their hearts they'll discover greater peace and satisfaction than they could ever imagine.

61

When He Needs to Stay Close to God

I am the true vine, and my Father is the gardener. He cuts off every branch in me that bears no fruit, while every branch that does bear fruit he prunes so that it will be even more fruitful. You are already clean because of the word I have spoken to you. Remain in me, as I also remain in you. No branch can bear fruit by itself; it must remain in the vine. Neither can you bear fruit unless you remain in me. I am the vine; you are the branches. If you remain in me and I in you, you will bear much fruit; apart from me you can do nothing.

John 15:1–5

Let us hold fast the confession of our hope without wavering, for he who promised is faithful.

Hebrews 10:23 ESV

L ORD,
My son believes that you are God. He understands that Christ's death on the cross has paid for his sins and made a way for him to be with you forever in heaven. He accepts the Bible as your Word. He goes to church, sings along to Christian music, and wants to live in obedience to you. I pray you would enable him to hold on to the faith he claims today for all the days of his life.

My son is young and his beliefs and trust in you have yet to be tested. He enjoys living by the rules and being told he's a "good kid." He has yet to wrestle with pain and loss that prayer did not remove. He hasn't had to resist strong temptation to sin and fit in with the world. He feels secure in his knowledge of you and is unaware of his own spiritual vulnerability.

Show my son how desperately he needs to abide in you. Write your Word on his heart and mind to defend him against the enemy's lies. Teach him to pray continually so he'll run to you with every question and concern. Give him a love for your church so your people can build him up in difficult times.

Keep my son from settling for an easy, shallow relationship with you. Let him wrestle with belief and trust until he makes his faith his own. Help him to lean on you when he's struggling. Let him find courage in you when he's afraid. When the world says the Bible is a myth and Jesus is merely a man, equip him to defend what he believes. Give him a heart that longs to please you in every way instead of conforming to the world around him.

Use me to encourage my son in following you. Give me wisdom to explain the Bible in a way he can understand. Make me faithful in prayer so we can experience your answers together. Help me to obey you in how I speak, serve, and love others so he can see you living in me. Don't let us become religious—going through the motions—but let our faith be powerful and alive.

Keep us close to you every day. Bear fruit in us as we hold on to your truth. Keep us from wavering, and make us more sure of you than anything else. Amen.

62

When He's Becoming Mature

When I was a child, I talked like a child, I thought like a child, I reasoned like a child. When I became a man, I put the ways of childhood behind me.

1 Corinthians 13:11

Then we will no longer be infants, tossed back and forth by the waves, and blown here and there by every wind of teaching and by the cunning and craftiness of people in their deceitful scheming. Instead, speaking the truth in love, we will grow to become in every respect the mature body of him who is the head, that is, Christ.

Ephesians 4:14–15

Let perseverance finish its work so that you may be mature and complete, not lacking anything. If any of you lacks wisdom, you should ask God, who gives generously to all without finding fault, and it will be given to you.

James 1:4–5

FATHER,
My son is feeling pulled between the exciting challenges of growing up and the easy life of childhood he's leaving behind. One moment he's playing outside or snitching cookies from the jar, and the next he's struggling with a homework assignment or building his savings account. He can become tired of the responsibilities and demands on his time as he grows. I see him moving backward instead of pressing on toward maturity.

Give my son wisdom to see the benefits of growing up. Open his eyes to see the opportunities and freedoms ahead. Help him to see that rewards are coming for the effort he's putting into studying, practicing, training, and working today. Let him experience the joy and respect that come from a job well done. Make him a helper that others can lean on so he can see his value and all he has to offer.

Help my son to grow up in his faith. Enable him to reach out to you without waiting for others to lead him. Kindle an interest in reading your Word for himself. Prompt him to pray and let him learn to hear your voice. Let him mature by making his faith his own, rather than just following a family tradition.

Develop my son's self-control so he can rise above his emotions. May he work and obey regardless of his feelings. Help him to control his temper. Give him strength to do the right thing even when he's battling temptation. Free him from a sense of entitlement and fill him with gratitude for all he's been given. Keep him from getting carried away with his friends so he can make responsible choices.

Give my son wisdom beyond his years. Let him have discernment by your Spirit to recognize any philosophy or message that contradicts your Word. May he choose his friends wisely, seeking those who bring out his best and support his faith in you. Give him humility to receive correction with a willing heart. Make him teachable and responsive to me and those in authority over him.

I love the imagination and creativity you've placed in my child. Help him to hold on to his curiosity, his energy, and his laughter as he grows. He finds joy in little things and has amazing dreams for the future. Guard his heart from losing trust that anything is possible with you. May he never lose his wonder over your creation. Keep him openhearted to the ones who love him the most.

Thank you for the gift of sharing my son's life, year by year. You are faithful in growing him into the amazing person you intend him to be. Help me to trust you by placing him in your hands, accepting your timing for how and when he reaches maturity. Amen.

63

When We Need Time Together

Be very careful, then, how you live—not as unwise but as wise, making the most of every opportunity, because the days are evil. Therefore do not be foolish, but understand what the Lord's will is.

Ephesians 5:15–17

There is a time for everything, and a season for every activity under the heavens: a time to be born and a time to die, a time to plant and a time to uproot, a time to kill and a time to heal, a time to tear down and a time to build, a time to weep and a time to laugh, a time to mourn and a time to dance, a time to scatter stones and a time to gather them, a time to embrace and a time to refrain from embracing, a time to search and a time to give up, a time to keep and a time to throw away, a time to tear and a time to mend, a time to be silent and a time to speak.

Ecclesiastes 3:1–7

FATHER GOD,
    This season of parenthood is busy and feels overwhelming. I am pulled in countless directions, feeling rushed and always behind. It's hard to live in the moment because I'm dwelling on my endless to-do list of things that need my attention. Sadly, I can forget to treasure my son. Connecting with him becomes crowded out by our busy schedule. I keep him clean, fed, and on task, but I don't always pause to look into his eyes and his heart.

Help me to remember that these days with him as a boy are fleeting. Guide me as I set my priorities, to make time to be still and listen to him and to you. Don't let me judge the value of my day merely by the work I've completed but by how I loved and connected with those you've placed in my life. Give me a passion to invest in relationships that will last for eternity.

Show me how to "make the most of every opportunity" by pointing my son to you in the ordinary moments of our life together. Let me lead him in prayer, enjoy your creation with him, and serve others together in your name. Remind me that you're more concerned with his character than his achievements. Let him be conformed to Christ instead of the crowd and cherished rather than spoiled. Help me to guard his heart and mind from anything that will take his eyes off you.

This is our time to grow, to draw near to each other and to you, and to discover your beautiful plans for my son. May we keep you in the center of everything we do together. Give him joy and security in me as I love him faithfully, like you love me. Let me know my son's heart and mind and praise your name for the person you've created him to be. Thank you for sharing this child with me—may I never take your gift for granted. Amen.

A Prayer Story

Not everything looks right with the sonogram" are frightening words to any parent, but when I was pregnant with our first child, a son we named George, we were living in England. Thousands of miles from home, we were feeling the normal anxieties of first-time parents, as well as dealing with an unfamiliar healthcare system. With just these few words from the doctor, we now faced the additional stress of caring for a sick child with an unknown future.

It was during that uncertain time that I was reading a book about the psalms. The author noted in Psalm 139, when David writes "certainly you made my mind and heart; you wove me together in my mother's womb" (v. 13 NET), that the word for *heart* in Hebrew is literally *kidneys*. To this day, I don't remember the name of the book or even the main point of the section I was reading. I didn't even read any further because I was completely overwhelmed by this almost unimportant comment about the literal meaning of a word in Psalm 139. George's kidneys were the organs that gave the doctors concern when they viewed the sonogram.

As I read and reread Psalm 139, I realized that it was a perfect expression of our situation. In verses 7–10, David writes, "Where can I go from your Spirit? Where can I flee from your presence? . . . If I settle on the far side of the sea, even there your hand will guide me, your right hand will hold me fast." I realized that God was reassuring me that on the far side of the Atlantic Ocean, that even in England, he would be present with us. I was comforted that in an unfamiliar place God would guide and strengthen us.

David continues in his psalm by praising God because he is "fearfully and wonderfully made; your works are wonderful, I know that full well" (v. 14). I was reminded that God was the one who had formed George's kidneys and we could trust him with his creation. In verse 16, David writes "all the days ordained for me were written in your book before one of them came to be." In those words, I received peace that God had fashioned each moment of George's life even before he was born.

As we endured two surgeries in the first few months of his life, as well as innumerable doctor and hospital visits, I was able to find comfort in the words of Psalm 139. It was this experience that began my journey of praying Scripture for George.

More than ten years later, I continue to regularly claim the promises of Psalm 139 for George. Now, I pray that George would know the reality of God's presence in his life (v. 8). I request for George to know he is a wonderful creation (v. 14). I pray that George would be able to claim God's thoughts as precious (v. 17) so that he would obey them. I intercede for George, asking the Lord to keep evil from him (v. 19). And I pray George would follow God in the way everlasting (v. 24).

In addition to Psalm 139, I regularly ask the Lord for Scripture verses for George (and my other children) to pray for him. Whether it is a certain situation or an area of his life that I would like to see God's power at work in him, I have found great power in praying the living, active, and transforming words of God directly into my son's life.

....

Married to Jim, **Lisa Samra** is a stay-at-home mom to their four children. Lisa also has the privilege to serve the Lord in a variety of capacities at Calvary Church in Grand Rapids, Michigan. To learn more about Lisa, see her blog at olivesandcoffee.calvarygr.org.

64

When He Needs to Find Rest

Be still, and know that I am God; I will be exalted among the nations, I will be exalted in the earth.

Psalm 46:10

Come to me, all who labor and are heavy laden, and I will give you rest. Take my yoke upon you, and learn from me, for I am gentle and lowly in heart, and you will find rest for your souls. For my yoke is easy, and my burden is light.

Matthew 11:28–30 ESV

The LORD is my shepherd; I shall not want. He makes me lie down in green pastures. He leads me beside still waters. He restores my soul.

Psalm 23:1–3 ESV

FATHER,
My son is tired. He's been working hard to learn, grow, and live up to what's expected of him. He feels like every moment of the day holds demands and responsibilities. He's not sure his efforts are enough—he's weary and needs help to keep going.

Academic pressures can make him insecure. He tries to study hard and stay organized, but assignments are still misplaced or come back with disappointing grades. He worries about losing the respect of his teachers. He looks at the success of other students and wonders if he'll measure up. Help him to keep on working without giving up. Give him wisdom to know how to manage his time and schoolwork. Clear away any confusion that's keeping him from understanding his lessons. Give him peace, knowing he's not loved by you or me because of his report card.

Outside of school, we can fill our calendar with team practices, music lessons, church activities, and social commitments. Give me wisdom as his parent to know when to slow down our pace. Show us your will for our schedule, and make us mindful before we say yes to any opportunity. Keep us from losing your best for us by filling our days with less important things. Help us to take moments to unplug and be still, so we can enjoy time together and with you.

Show me how to minister to my son when he's weary. Give me a gentle, helpful spirit to care for him and build him up when he's discouraged. Help me to slow down and listen if he needs to vent about his day. Keep me from pressuring him to perform. Let him experience your grace through me as I accept him just as he is.

The pressures of this world can be heavy to carry. Thank you that we can rest in you. You care for every need and pick us up when we fall. Draw near to my son right now so he can feel your love. Give him strength to face tomorrow. Amen.

65

When He's Attacked by the Enemy

Be alert and of sober mind. Your enemy the devil prowls around like a roaring lion looking for someone to devour. Resist him, standing firm in the faith, because you know that the family of believers throughout the world is undergoing the same kind of sufferings.

1 Peter 5:8–9

Submit yourselves, then, to God. Resist the devil, and he will flee from you.

James 4:7

Finally, be strong in the Lord and in his mighty power. Put on the full armor of God, so that you can take your stand against the devil's schemes. For our struggle is not against flesh and blood, but against the rulers, against the authorities, against the powers of this dark world and against the spiritual forces of evil in the heavenly realms. Therefore put on the full armor of God, so that when the day of evil comes, you may be able to stand your ground, and after you have done everything, to stand.

Ephesians 6:10–13

FATHER,

My son has a beautiful heart and is a precious gift from you. He has been my treasure since the day he was born. It's hard to comprehend an evil enemy who is determined to destroy my child. Yet I see the darkness of this world and know he'll experience attacks on every side.

The devil will lie to my son and tell him he's worthless. Give my son confidence in your love and the truth that he's created in the image of God himself. Open his eyes to the abilities and talents you're developing in him even now. Show my son what a gift he can be to this world—you may use him to relieve suffering, teach your truth, and give hope to those in despair—so he can know that his life has great purpose.

The enemy will try to destroy him through sin. Give my son strength to overcome lust, dishonesty, greed, deceit, and anger. Make him faithful to obey you and those in authority in his life. Let him walk in integrity at school, work, and home. Keep him pure and devoted to his loved ones. Guard his innocence and give him the courage to stand for what is right.

Satan will try to harm his health and safety. Protect my son from violence and danger. When others give in to rage, crime, or alcohol or drug abuse, spare my son from suffering for their foolish choices. Sustain his physical health and guard him from disease or injuries that could bring him down. Keep watch over him so he can live a long life of serving and following you.

Most of all, keep the enemy from tearing down his trust in you. Help my son to believe the promises of your Word so he can count on your forgiveness and mercy. Sustain his confidence that his prayers are heard and answered. Let him hold to what you say is right and wrong so he doesn't violate his conscience or deny your Holy Spirit. Give him assurance that the Scriptures are your perfect Word. When he suffers through difficulties, never let him doubt how good and loving you truly are.

Teach my son to put on your armor—your truth, righteousness, the gospel of peace, faith, salvation, and your Spirit—so the enemy has no power against him. Give him victory over every lie and temptation that comes his way. Let him stand for you every day of his life, until we see you face-to-face. Amen.

66

When He's Discovering His Spiritual Gifts

There are different kinds of gifts, but the same Spirit distributes them. There are different kinds of service, but the same Lord. There are different kinds of working, but in all of them and in everyone it is the same God at work. Now to each one the manifestation of the Spirit is given for the common good.

1 Corinthians 12:4–7

Just as each of us has one body with many members, and these members do not all have the same function, so in Christ we, though many, form one body, and each member belongs to all the others. We have different gifts, according to the grace given to each of us. If your gift is prophesying, then prophesy in accordance with your faith; if it is serving, then serve; if it is teaching, then teach; if it is to encourage, then give encouragement; if it is giving, then give generously; if it is to lead, do it diligently; if it is to show mercy, do it cheerfully.

Romans 12:4–8

F ATHER,
In your great wisdom you created a family of believers, made up of individuals with unique and wonderful gifts. You bless us through one another's encouragement, insight, help, generosity, and teaching of your Word. You promised that every one of us would have a special gift to offer—we each have a place in your kingdom and each of us matter.

Thank you for how you are equipping my son to serve your people and join in your work in this world. Give my son the joy of discovering his spiritual gifts from you. If his gifts are compassion and giving, use him to relieve suffering and poverty. If he has musical ability, let him lead your people in worship and praise. If he has wisdom and knowledge, let him share your Word and influence others for Christ. If he is creative and skilled with his hands, let him repair and build in your service. If he's an encourager, may he give hope to those in defeat and despair.

Use my son's spiritual gifts to assure him of your presence in his life. Open doors for him to help and give of himself to others. Let him discover the joy of serving in your name. Guard his heart from trusting in his own abilities, for you are the source of all his strength. May he use his gifts to glorify you instead of seeking recognition for himself. Give him a humble heart as you enable him to minister to others in amazing ways.

Show me how to support my son in serving you. Give me insight into the gifts you're developing in him. Teach me how to exercise my own spiritual gifts so I can set an example of ministry before him.

Thank you for allowing us to love others in your name. May we offer every talent, passion, and gift we have to you, to use for your glory. Amen.

67

When He's Critical of Others

Do not judge, or you too will be judged. For in the same way you judge others, you will be judged, and with the measure you use, it will be measured to you. Why do you look at the speck of sawdust in your brother's eye and pay no attention to the plank in your own eye? How can you say to your brother, "Let me take the speck out of your eye," when all the time there is a plank in your own eye?

Matthew 7:1–4

For by the grace given me I say to every one of you: Do not think of yourself more highly than you ought, but rather think of yourself with sober judgment, in accordance with the faith God has distributed to each of you.

Romans 12:3

Be completely humble and gentle; be patient, bearing with one another in love. Make every effort to keep the unity of the Spirit through the bond of peace.

Ephesians 4:2–3

FATHER,
My son needs to view others the way you see us. When you look at us, you see Jesus instead of our sin and failure. When we received your salvation, you declared us righteous. You are making us new from

the inside out. You give us a new identity as your beloved children, your temple, your witnesses, your friends, and your light in the world.

Help my son to focus on his own behavior and choices instead of judging everyone else. It's easy for him to point fingers at the disrespectful student in his class, the teammate who's lazy at practice, the brother or sister whose room is a mess, or the young person at church with a bad attitude. Let him remember the times that he, too, has been careless or selfish, angry or rude. We "all have sinned and fall short of the glory of God," and are helpless to change without the work of your Spirit (Rom. 3:23).

You are working in us day by day to purify our hearts from sin and renew our minds to think like Christ. You are so patient—when we make the same mistakes over and over, you never give up or let us go. I pray that my son would be able to show that same patience with everyone around him.

Guard our family from tearing one another down through critical attitudes. Let us show grace to one another when we fail. Help us to bear with each other, trusting that you're doing your perfecting work in each of us day by day. Let us show mercy and forgiveness to each other and everyone you bring through our door. Make our home a place of acceptance and love for all.

Use me as an example to my son in how I speak of others. When I'm driving, let me be gracious if another driver cuts me off. Make me patient at the store if the cashier is slow or inexperienced. Keep me from two-faced friendships where I'm warm and polite in person but pick them apart after they've gone home. Give me an understanding heart for those in authority over me instead of complaining about their leadership style. Make me patient with messes, mistakes, and annoyances at home so my family feels your grace through me.

Give my son your heart of love that builds others up and seeks peace with everyone. Thank you for accepting my son and working in his life to make him like Jesus. You are our hope and our joy. Amen.

68

When He Feels Pressure to Fit In

Do not conform to the pattern of this world, but be transformed by the renewing of your mind. Then you will be able to test and approve what God's will is—his good, pleasing and perfect will.

Romans 12:2

Follow God's example, therefore, as dearly loved children and walk in the way of love, just as Christ loved us and gave himself up for us as a fragrant offering and sacrifice to God.

Ephesians 5:1–2

The LORD does not look at the things people look at. People look at the outward appearance, but the LORD looks at the heart.

1 Samuel 16:7

LORD,
     My son feels the pull to speak, look, and behave like the boys around him. He's tempted to fall into the same rude language and disrespectful attitudes they express. He's invited to watch movies or play video games that don't match up with our family's values. He's concerned about having the right haircut and purchasing brand-name clothing and shoes. He's worried about having the latest devices everyone else seems to be buying. He's encouraged to idolize celebrities and sports figures, no matter their lifestyle or character. He's pressured to blend in with the group, putting down or leaving out any child who's different or not as popular. He needs your help to stay true to you and who *you* say he is in Christ.

     Teach my son to imitate you instead of the people around him. Give him your eyes that focus on the inner character, attitudes, and faith of others instead of their appearance and possessions. Let him pursue friendships based on honesty, respect, and integrity rather than using people to boost his social status.

Renew my son's mind to know right from wrong. Give him courage to obey you even if no one else does. Let him "walk in the way of love" by reaching out to kids who are alone. May he surrender his efforts to fit in and submit to others' expectations so he can put all his energy into living for you.

I pray you would reward my son with meaningful relationships and the respect of others as he stands firm in you. Use him as an example of excellent conduct among his peers. Keep him from discouragement on the days he feels misunderstood or put down for standing out. Show me how to encourage him and build him up. Help me to faithfully remind him that he is yours, for he is loved "with an everlasting love" (Jer. 31:3).

Keep my son secure and close to you. Thank you for your wonderful promises to claim him as your own and call him your child. I praise you for cherishing my son's heart and loving him forever. Amen.

His Relationship with God

Hear, O Israel: The LORD our God, the LORD is one. Love the LORD your God with all your heart and with all your soul and with all your strength. These commandments that I give you today are to be on your hearts. Impress them on your children. Talk about them when you sit at home and when you walk along the road, when you lie down and when you get up. Tie them as symbols on your hands and bind them on your foreheads. Write them on the doorframes of your houses and on your gates.

Deuteronomy 6:4–9

A child will not accept a life plan to which his parents only give mental assent. If a child is going to accept your faith as his own, he must see it lived out. Alive and breathing and functioning. In YOU!

Dr. Tim Kimmel[8]

As parents we have an endless list of responsibilities. Shopping. Driving. Cleaning. Working. Teaching. Budgeting. Planning. But while we're serving our families in a wide variety of ways, our absolute highest purpose is to introduce our kids to God. Through our words and example, our boys need to hear the truth of who God is and how much he loves them.

Our greatest desire for our sons should be that they place their trust in God. To understand the gospel message as it reveals the work of Christ and how they can be saved. To love the Lord with all their soul and mind and strength (Mark 12:30). Any other hopes we have for our boys are meaningless compared to knowing their Savior.

It's difficult, however, because there are so many ideas and opinions about how parents should train their children in the faith. It can be overwhelming to know what to do. In addition, we have hectic schedules that make it hard to fit in family devotions, Bible reading, and prayer. I believe most Christian parents walk around carrying guilt that they're not doing enough to pass their faith on to their children.

That is why I love the passage in Deuteronomy 6. It describes how we can talk about God's truth "when you sit at home and when you walk along the road, when you lie down and when you get up" (v. 7). It gives us a wonderful model of how parents can encourage their kids along in their own faith walk. We can use the little moments of every day to show them that our relationship with God is not just a thirty-minute quiet time in the morning or saying grace before supper. It's experiencing the presence and power of God in the everyday moments of life with our children.

If we love the Lord with all of our heart, soul, and might, it shows in our obedience throughout the day. We demonstrate God's faithfulness when our kids can count on us to drive them to school on time with clean clothes and a full lunch box. We can talk about humility and serving others when we're coming home from a disappointing soccer game. We can share how God is our strength to depend on when they're struggling to keep their grades up. When we pray with them at bedtime we can encourage gratitude by praising the Lord for all he's done for us in the last twenty-four hours.

We have found that mealtime offers one of the best opportunities for us to connect as a family and talk about our faith. We have "highs and lows," where each of us takes a turn sharing how God gave an unexpected blessing and where we struggled and needed his help. The table is a place to practice honoring each other by turning off our phones and listening to what each other has to say.

The dinner hour is also where we've found the most consistency with Bible reading as a family. We keep a small basket handy that holds a copy of the Word for each of us. We take turns reading the verses for the day's passage, with everyone reading along as we go. Our kids have a chance to share which verse in the passage really speaks to them, and why. It's a special way to learn from each other and share from our heart.

We can put a lot of pressure on ourselves, feeling that it's our job to save our children. While God encourages us to live our faith before our kids and teach them his Word, their salvation ultimately comes from him. We can rest in knowing he is fully able to reach our sons' hearts and give them new life. As Jesus said, "With man this is impossible, but not with God; all things are possible with God" (Mark 10:27). It encourages us to know our kids are in his hands—we can trust God to reveal himself in a real way and to help them remain faithful in following him.

We also pray for help to live a godly life before our children. They can see through our double standards or if we're just living to please ourselves. They will become disillusioned with Christianity if we reduce it to a list of dos and don'ts. We pray we'll live in obedience in every area and surrender our lives to God's control. The book *Sticky Faith* puts it well: "Model for your children that, more than just a worldview or a way of life, Christianity is first and foremost an intimate relationship with the Father."[9]

When we pray about our parenting, we ask for help to stay diligent in studying the Word so our children will know it's our source of wisdom and values. We ask for strength to work and serve even when we're tired. We ask to be filled with unconditional love for our boys that mirrors the love of God himself. We pray that our spiritual walk will be more about worship than just following the rules. We want our sons to see authenticity, where what we say matches how we live. We ask for undivided hearts that love God above anything the world has to offer.

God has given us some awesome promises to encourage us along the way. He says he "has blessed us in the heavenly realms with every spiritual blessing in Christ" (Eph. 1:3). And he tells us that "His divine power has given us everything we need for a godly life through our knowledge of him who called us by his own glory and goodness" (2 Pet. 1:3). Even when we're feeling like spiritual failures, those verses let us know that God can give us everything we need to raise our sons. They remind us that the burden isn't on our own shoulders, because apart from God we can do nothing (John 15:5). He gives us strength when we feel inadequate. He gives peace even when our sons are struggling with unbelief and disobedience. Our God is the One who runs to embrace the prodigal. He is the Good Shepherd who leaves the ninety-nine sheep to go out and find the single one that's lost. Be assured that God loves your son and is mighty and willing to rescue him.

Since God has given us all of those spiritual blessings, we are excited to share them with our children. We can commit to a local church so our son experiences a body of believers who care for him. We can open the Word and study so he hears what God has to say. Our house rules can reflect the perfect ways of God by encouraging kindness and respect. We can share God's grace through a forgiving spirit that never turns them away. We can enjoy worship together, praying and singing along with music in the car. We can find the joy of serving others as a family by helping those around us. We can celebrate God together whenever we say thanks for how he's blessed our family.

Be at peace, knowing your son can see that God is alive by how he lives in you. Your love, your help, and your wisdom are gifts from God to your son today. Keep on praying and trusting the Lord to reach your son's heart at the perfect time. "The one who calls you is faithful, and he will do it" (1 Thess. 5:24).

69

When He's Discontent

I know what it is to be in need, and I know what it is to have plenty. I have learned the secret of being content in any and every situation, whether well fed or hungry, whether living in plenty or in want. I can do all this through him who gives me strength.

Philippians 4:12–13

Rejoice always, pray continually, give thanks in all circumstances; for this is God's will for you in Christ Jesus.

1 Thessalonians 5:16–18

This is the day that the LORD has made; let us rejoice and be glad in it. . . . Oh give thanks to the LORD, for he is good; for his steadfast love endures forever!

Psalm 118:24, 29 ESV

F ATHER,
     I pray that my son would discover the "secret of being content."
It can be a struggle even though you have filled our lives with too
many blessings to count. We have wholesome food and safe shelter,
work that brings purpose to our day, and the love of friends and family. We have your Word and your church to encourage us in every
situation. We never walk through life alone because you promise to
be with us always. There aren't enough hours in a day to thank you
for all you've done.

In our foolishness and selfishness, however, we still find ourselves
wanting what we do not have. If my son is busy he'll wish he could
relax, but if the day is quiet he finds himself restless and bored. He'd
rather I spend money on wants instead of needs. He can resist sharing
what he has with others, but is resentful if others withhold generosity
from him. His heart is divided—he loves me and you and is grateful
for what he's given, but he craves what he can see with his eyes. He's
never fully satisfied.

Give my son a thankful heart that doesn't take even the most
simple gift for granted. Strengthen him with patience to wait for
the possessions and experiences he's eager to obtain. Help him to
trust you to bring exactly what is best for him at the perfect time.

When my son has to do without and when his needs or desires are
delayed in coming, let him lean on you. Give him strength to endure
hardship without complaining or doubting your goodness. Use any
struggles he suffers through to create compassion for others who are
hurting. Give him a generous heart to gladly share what he has.

Keep my heart from any greed or discontentment that could cause
my son to stumble. Give me opportunities to give and share with
others, living out a selfless attitude for my son to follow. Make me a
patient, grateful parent who acknowledges your goodness to our family. May I see my son as a gift from you and accept him just as he is. Let
me show grace to him and rejoice that you've shared his life with me.

You are good, and your love endures forever. Amen.

70

When He Doubts His Own Worth

But you are a chosen people, a royal priesthood, a holy nation, God's special possession, that you may declare the praises of him who called you out of darkness into his wonderful light.

1 Peter 2:9

Are not five sparrows sold for two pennies? Yet not one of them is forgotten by God. Indeed, the very hairs of your head are all numbered. Don't be afraid; you are worth more than many sparrows.

Luke 12:6–7

But he said to me, "My grace is sufficient for you, for my power is made perfect in weakness." Therefore I will boast all the more gladly about my weaknesses, so that Christ's power may rest on me. That is why, for Christ's sake, I delight in weaknesses, in insults, in hardships, in persecutions, in difficulties. For when I am weak, then I am strong.

2 Corinthians 12:9–10

FATHER,
My son is afraid he's not good enough. He worries about everything—is he handsome or ugly? Smart or stupid? Athletic or clumsy? Popular or rejected? Funny or boring? At the end of the day, he's not sure he has what it takes to please other people or even you.

I hear so many comments from my son about how he has failed or feels embarrassed. He gets frustrated with me if I ask him to study or work at anything where he feels weak. He takes teasing or any word of criticism too much to heart. He takes his insecurity out on his family and friends, criticizing or insulting in a feeble attempt to make himself feel bigger or better. He is listening to the enemy's lies that he's worthless. He has forgotten how valuable he is in your eyes.

Fill my son's mind with the truth that he has been created by you and chosen to be your child. Remind him that you are with him all the time, ready to help whenever he's feeling weak. Help him to find security in your grace and acceptance so he's free from the pressure to please other people.

Teach my son that he was put on this earth to "declare the praises of him who called you out of darkness into his wonderful light." No matter how successful or impressive he may become, his true calling is to show how perfect and awesome *you* are.

Comfort my son in his failure. Help him to see his imperfections as a wonderful chance to experience your strength. Give him trust in your Word that says, "My grace is sufficient for you, for my power is made perfect in weakness." Let him learn to depend on you when he's reached the limits of his own abilities. Encourage him that with your help, anything is possible.

Set my son's mind free from focusing on his own self-image. Take his eyes off of himself so he can dwell on how good you are. Help him to appreciate the talents and blessings others have without becoming jealous or competitive. Give him peace that he's special and loved just as he is today, so he can give that same grace to the people in his life.

Thank you for being the source of every talent, strength, and gift we possess. Let us worship you for your faithful work to make us new day by day. We are not who we once were without you, and we are not yet who we'll become when you bring us home. May we rest in your love every moment. Amen.

71

When I'm Losing Hope in My Son

Love is patient, love is kind. It does not envy, it does not boast, it is not proud. It does not dishonor others, it is not self-seeking, it is not easily angered, it keeps no record of wrongs. Love does not delight in evil but rejoices with the truth. It always protects, always trusts, always hopes, always perseveres. Love never fails.

1 Corinthians 13:4–8

Be completely humble and gentle; be patient, bearing with one another in love. Make every effort to keep the unity of the Spirit through the bond of peace.

Ephesians 4:2–3

FATHER,
I'm struggling to *like* my son, even though I *love* him so deeply. He's negative, he's disorganized, he's unmotivated, and he's stubborn. He makes foolish choices that bring difficult consequences, but he doesn't learn from his mistakes. No matter how gentle or harsh, sensitive or stern I am, it doesn't seem like anything I say makes a difference in his life. I'm at my wit's end and I feel like giving up.

Help me to forgive my son as you have forgiven me. You are a God of second chances and you want me to have mercy on my son. Help me to bear with him, trusting you'll work in his heart at exactly the right time.

Keep me from quitting my job as his parent. Help me to stay faithful in speaking the truth and disciplining him when he needs correction. Let me train him wisely, rather than just punishing him out of anger. Give me courage to give him what he needs instead of just what he wants. Show me what words he needs to hear and what privileges to remove as you lead him to repentance.

Remind me that he is your creation, made in your image. Give me a fresh perspective to enjoy his personality and recognize his strengths. Help me to see what he's doing right and how he's growing so I can praise him and build him up. Keep me from speaking negatively of him to others, even when I'm tired or frustrated. Fill my heart with compassion and understanding, knowing that his weaknesses will create pain and difficulty in his life. Bind us together in peace by your Spirit—able to value one another and let go of the past.

Teach me what true love looks like. Give me a servant's heart to keep helping and giving with a cheerful attitude, even if it feels one-sided. Help me to hold on to hope for him. Build my faith to believe you're in control. He's in your hands, not mine. Your Spirit will do the work that's needed to bring him to maturity.

Draw close to my son today. Let him sense your presence and the love you freely offer. Speak to him through your Word, your people, and me. Thank you for what you will do in my son's life. And thank you for using this difficult season with my son to increase my patience and faith in you. Amen.

72

When He Has a Negative Attitude

Do everything without grumbling or arguing, so that you may become blameless and pure, "children of God without fault in a warped and crooked generation." Then you will shine among them like stars in the sky.

Philippians 2:14–15

What causes fights and quarrels among you? Don't they come from your desires that battle within you? You desire but do not have, so you kill. You covet but you cannot get what you want, so you quarrel and fight. You do not have because you do not ask God.

James 4:1–2

Why, my soul, are you downcast? Why so disturbed within me? Put your hope in God, for I will yet praise him, my Savior and my God.

Psalm 42:11

LORD,
My son is struggling deeply with his attitude. He feels cheated, as if everyone around him has it better than he does. He complains about having to work and argues over everything I ask him to do. He's easily irritated and doesn't seem to enjoy spending time with our family. He's becoming more disrespectful and negative each day.

I'm walking on eggshells around him, not knowing what will set him off. I find myself expecting less and less of him, since he doesn't like to help and doesn't do a good job anyway. His negativity and bad moods are isolating him from our family, and affecting his interest in the Lord as well. He needs your help to restore his smile, his joy, and his love.

If my son is resentful of the privileges or possessions that his siblings and friends have, create a grateful heart in him that can appreciate his gifts. Open his eyes to the struggles and pain of others so he can recognize how blessed he truly is. If his dark moods are caused by the guilt of secret sin he's holding on to, let him find forgiveness and peace in you. If he's been hurt by someone's words or actions, give him courage to share what happened so he can receive comfort and help. Soften his heart so he can forgive anyone who's offended him.

If my son is worried, betrayed, confused, or frustrated about something in his life, I pray he would experience your hope and peace. Let him reach out to you in prayer and discover that you hear and respond. Use this hard season to show him how near you are—eager to help and full of love.

Give me patience and compassion for my son. Show me how to hold him accountable for his behavior while encouraging him at the same time. Keep his negativity from stealing the joy and laughter from our household. Let me respond to his complaining with thanksgiving, his anger with a gentle spirit, and his resistance with strength. Help us to get through this and bring us closer together in the end.

Thank you for your great mercy that bears with us when we're struggling. Your love never fails. Amen.

73

When He Needs Motivation

His divine power has given us everything we need for a godly life through our knowledge of him who called us by his own glory and goodness. Through these he has given us his very great and precious promises, so that through them you may participate in the divine nature, having escaped the corruption in the world caused by evil desires. For this very reason, make every effort to add to your faith goodness; and to goodness, knowledge; and to knowledge, self-control; and to self-control, perseverance; and to perseverance, godliness; and to godliness, mutual affection; and to mutual affection, love. For if you possess these qualities in increasing measure, they will keep you from being ineffective and unproductive in your knowledge of our Lord Jesus Christ.

2 Peter 1:3–8

He gives strength to the weary and increases the power of the weak. Even youths grow tired and weary, and young men stumble and fall;

but those who hope in the LORD will renew their strength. They will soar on wings like eagles; they will run and not grow weary, they will walk and not be faint.

Isaiah 40:29–31

FATHER,
Growing up is hard work. It takes energy to tackle challenging schoolwork, develop athletic or musical skills, complete projects, and finish chores every day. When the to-do list is difficult or boring it's even harder to face. My son is losing his motivation to press on and do his best at the tasks at hand. He needs your help to persevere.

My son can become too focused on the outcome of his work. He's tempted to reject any activity where he feels inferior. Give him endurance to practice in areas where he's weak so he can grow in his abilities. Guard him from a competitive attitude that's only satisfied with winning or being the best.

Protect my son from the weaknesses of laziness or apathy. Let him discover the truth that we are working to please you, not other people. Give him satisfaction in knowing that you recognize his efforts even if no one else can see them. When he's giving up on ever receiving a reward for his labor, give him peace in knowing you see everything and hold eternal rewards in your hand.

Awaken my son's mind and spark a fresh curiosity to learn and explore. Keep him from wasting his energy and attention on useless things. Let him place value on relationships over relaxation and experience over entertainment so that his days hold purpose and meaning.

While it's important that my son pursue strong academics and work well done, may his greatest purpose lie in serving you. When he's tired of standing out from the crowd by holding on to his faith alone, give him strength to stand firm. When he's tempted to give in to sinful desires, let him run to you and find strength to obey. If the Bible seems too complicated to understand, may he read it again and again until it speaks to his heart.

Give my son eagerness to experience the abundant life you promise. Shake him out of his apathy to discover all you have in store if he perseveres. Show me how to encourage him as he finds his way. Amen.

A Prayer Story

When I was pregnant with my second child, I prayed for a son and God heard and answered my prayers. As my son grew I continually prayed with him and for him. As much as I had hoped to save him from ever getting hurt, some lessons he would need to learn the hard way and some hurts he would need Jesus to heal.

From the time he was just a little boy he loved football. He was always on the field or in the locker room with his dad, the coach of the high school team. It was inevitable that my son would have a strong desire to play. His football career began in the fourth grade, and his place as the team quarterback began the following year. He was one of the youngest kids in his class and one of the smaller players on the field. Each game it seemed as though the opposing players grew bigger and bigger and my prayers for my son grew with them!

In high school, his first two years on the junior varsity team earned a successful season with him as quarterback and only increased his love for the game. He couldn't wait to be on the varsity team, and he dreamed of one day playing at the college level and even playing in the NFL.

Faith was always a big part of his life. The summer prior to his first varsity season, he went on a mission trip to Guatemala. It was a life-changing event for him as he carried fifty-pound baskets of food to remote villages in the mountains. It was a test of my faith as I allowed my youngest child—my son—to travel to another country.

Once again God answered my prayers and brought him home safely with a renewed spirit.

Once he returned, his football season began with "two-a-days," a tough few weeks of practice before the actual games began. He had been treated for back pain on and off, but nothing seemed serious until he came home from practice one day in so much pain that we knew we needed to get some answers quickly.

After a CT scan, an MRI, and a bone scan, the source of his tremendous pain was found as they discovered four fractures in his spine. There were four cracks all in a row, so it would only have taken one good hit for everything to change in his life. The injury was so unheard of that the specialist actually used it as a study.

That was it. His football season, and quite possibly his football career, were over as he was fitted for a back brace that he would wear for the next several months. To be honest, I'm not sure which was more broken, his heart or his back. My heart was broken too.

We were both so grateful that God had spared him from a greater injury that could have resulted in complete paralysis or worse, and we tried to focus on that rather than the great disappointment in the loss of his plans and dreams. Yet it was difficult to see him in so much pain, standing there on the sidelines watching his team play without him, game after game.

All I could do was pray and so I did. I prayed God would give him strength and heal all his brokenness. At one point during his healing he confessed to me that his faith was more important to him than football. He continued to believe that he would one day be healed and whole.

After a long football season, it was back to the specialist, who was amazed at his progress and gave him the "all clear" to play again. I was not so certain, and reminded him of his injury and what could happen. He replied, "Mom, Jesus healed my back. It's healed, stronger than before." I had been praying and believing too, so I let go of my fears and trusted, and continued to pray as the next football season began. In his senior year, with my son as quarterback, his team broke school records as they made it into the playoffs. They went farther than any team ever had before in our small town. God had answered our prayers!

As he prepared to graduate that year, he visited a few colleges and spoke with coaches about playing football. It was all so exciting, and our prayers for direction were continually answered as he settled on a school that had a great football program and was only a couple of hours away. His college plans secure, with scholarships and grants, we waited for this new chapter in his life to begin.

Then came the news that would completely break my heart. My son, a high school senior, was going to be a dad. I was devastated as I thought of all his plans and dreams that would surely be destroyed. Once again I prayed, believing God would help him, and help us, through this.

Although he didn't readily admit it, he was scared and disappointed and sure he had cancelled any good plans God had for him. After much discussion and prayer, it was decided that he would continue with his plans to go to college. If he was going to be a dad he would also need to be a provider. We moved him to his new home in the freshman dorms just as football practices were beginning.

We assumed as a freshman he wouldn't see a lot of playing time, especially as quarterback, considering there were well over one hundred players on his team. We were wrong. He played. A lot. Not only did he play almost every game, but they won the playoffs that year. In his freshman year of college as quarterback he earned a championship ring—only God!

God is faithful even when we're not. My son's first college football season quickly came to an amazing end and now we awaited the birth of a baby girl. Several weeks later the call arrived, and we headed to the hospital. One look into her beautiful face was all it took, and we were captivated. God blesses us in spite of our choices; his plans for us are not deterred.

My son made the decision to transfer to a college that was closer to home to be near his daughter. He is a wonderful, loving father and I can't imagine our lives without his precious little girl. God has answered my prayers for my son over and over again. He turns what is broken into something beautiful.

....

Lanette Haskins is a wife, mom, and "grammy" to her granddaughters and resides with her family in Michigan. She is a writer at *Grace Found Me*, www.lanettehaskins.blogspot.com; and leads a ministry, Healing for the Abortion Wounded Heart.

74

When He's in the Wrong Crowd

Even a child makes himself known by his acts, by whether his conduct is pure and upright.

Proverbs 20:11 ESV

Do not be misled: "Bad company corrupts good character." Come back to your senses as you ought, and stop sinning; for there are some who are ignorant of God—I say this to your shame.

1 Corinthians 15:33–34

Walk with the wise and become wise, for a companion of fools suffers harm.

Proverbs 13:20

L ORD,
My son is being led down a destructive path by the group of friends he's a part of. He's letting others influence his belief in what's right and wrong. His faith is shaken by their criticism of you and your Word. His obedience and conscience are becoming compromised by his pursuit of fun and acceptance. He's lost his way, and he needs help to find his way back to you.

I pray that my son would "come back to his senses" and remember that you are the one true God. Help him to remember what is right and wrong—may he turn away from his sin and submit to you in everything. He's making choices and speaking words that deny his identity as your child. He's beginning to experience the painful consequences of going his own way. Let him rediscover his true self as a chosen, beloved follower of Jesus.

Surround my son with men of God who will challenge him to commit to you. Let him "walk with the wise" and see your power and love lived out through others. Give him the courage to turn away from friendship with anyone who would deny you or encourage him to disobey your Word. Lead him into fellowship with other believers so he doesn't have to live out his fragile faith alone.

I pray my son would trust fully in your forgiveness. Guard his mind from believing that he's wandered too far to reach you again. Let him discover you as his best friend—a companion that's always beside him, whose love never fails.

Give me a heart of compassion for his friends. Replace my anger and frustration with love and concern for how much they need you. Show me how to reach out in love while helping my son to guard himself from their influence. Make our home a place where your light shines, so they see *you* when they're with us.

Give me faith to believe you will deliver my son from the wrong crowd. Help me to be patient and full of grace as you work in his life. Thank you for loving my son and never giving up on him. Amen.

75

When He's Competitive

Do nothing out of selfish ambition or vain conceit. Rather, in humility value others above yourselves.

Philippians 2:3

For everything in the world—the lust of the flesh, the lust of the eyes, and the pride of life—comes not from the Father but from the world. The world and its desires pass away, but whoever does the will of God lives forever.

1 John 2:16–17

So whether you eat or drink or whatever you do, do it all for the glory of God.

1 Corinthians 10:31

FATHER,
My son loves to win! He has a drive to play hard, practice with all his strength, and come out on top in competition. He needs your help, though, to compete with a godly attitude.

Guard my son's heart from pride that wants to outperform everyone else. Give him humility to build up his teammates and encourage success for everyone. Let him put the team first instead of chasing glory for himself. Let him submit to his coach's instruction and show respect for the officials.

I pray that my son would have the heart of a servant to his team and to you. If he strives for excellence, may it be to please you and benefit the group. Give him an appreciation for the talents of others with an understanding of his own weaknesses.

Keep my son from boasting about his achievements. May he be still and allow any reward or praise to come from others and from you. Give him a gracious, honorable attitude toward the losing team. When it's not his day to succeed, keep him from becoming a sore loser. Let him accept the outcome and determine to do his best no matter what.

I pray that my son would live his life to make your name great. If he's training, competing, saving up money to buy equipment, welcoming a new team member, or taking hard correction from a coach, let his motivation be to love and live like Jesus. Give him patience and endurance when he feels like quitting. Make him a peacemaker when his team is divided. Keep him positive and supportive in times of disappointment.

Show me how to support my son in competition. Govern my heart so I value his conduct more than his trophies. Let me set an example of respect and godliness in how I interact with the team parents and coaches. Use me as an encouragement and a peacemaker. Give me wisdom to balance our time so that family relationships and worship are not lost to practices and schedules.

Thank you for using competition to stretch and mature my son. Let him know your will and eagerly obey you in everything. Be glorified in him all the days of his life. Amen.

76

When He's Managing His Money

Those who want to get rich fall into temptation and a trap and into many foolish and harmful desires that plunge people into ruin and destruction. For the love of money is a root of all kinds of evil. Some people, eager for money, have wandered from the faith and pierced themselves with many griefs.

1 Timothy 6:9–10

Do not be afraid, little flock, for your Father has been pleased to give you the kingdom. Sell your possessions and give to the poor. Provide purses for yourselves that will not wear out, a treasure in heaven that will never fail, where no thief comes near and no moth destroys. For where your treasure is, there your heart will be also.

Luke 12:32–34

No one can serve two masters. Either you will hate the one and love the other, or you will be devoted to the one and despise the other. You cannot serve both God and money.

Matthew 6:24

FATHER,
Our money and resources are a gift from you. In your goodness you reward our work through our earnings. You provide the means to maintain our household and care for our physical needs. You enable us to share what we have with others, to relieve poverty and accomplish your mission to the world. However, money can become a destructive trap when we depend on it for our security and happiness.

Give my son a wise perspective on his finances. Help him to recognize how you've provided for him and to praise you for your gifts. May he be content with all he has. Keep him free from the lie that he can find happiness in material things rather than you. Guard him from a greedy heart that will never be satisfied and refuses to be generous.

Give my son wisdom and strength to work diligently and save what he earns. Give him the creativity and perseverance to increase his bank account as he grows. May he be mindful in how he spends his money—give him patience and discernment to avoid foolish spending that he'll regret.

Let my son discover the joy to be found in giving generously to others. Keep him from hoarding what he has, understanding that your blessings are meant to be freely shared. Help him to find his security in you and your faithfulness, rather than his own abilities and bank balance.

May I be an example of obedience and wisdom as I manage the resources you provide. Give me self-control in my spending, wisdom in my savings and investments, and a heart that's eager to share with everyone. Most of all, give me a spirit of thankfulness and gratitude for all you've done for us.

Thank you for your faithfulness in meeting our needs. May we seek our treasure in you and you alone. Amen.

77

When I Don't Know What to Pray

We know that the whole creation has been groaning as in the pains of childbirth right up to the present time. Not only so, but we ourselves, who have the firstfruits of the Spirit, groan inwardly as we wait eagerly for our adoption to sonship, the redemption of our bodies. For in this hope we were saved. But hope that is seen is no hope at all. Who hopes for what they already have? But if we hope for what we do not yet have, we wait for it patiently. In the same way, the Spirit helps us in our weakness. We do not know what we ought to pray for, but the Spirit himself intercedes for us through wordless groans. And he who searches our hearts knows the mind of the Spirit, because the Spirit intercedes for God's people in accordance with the will of God.

Romans 8:22–27

FATHER,
I don't know how to pray for my son. All I know for certain
is that he needs you. This world is full of pain, violence, and sin. It
seems like a foolish wish to hope that my son will be able to know
you and walk in your ways. Today, when I'm confused and doubtful
that he'll find his way, I trust that you *know*.

Thank you for your Spirit who prays for my son when he can't pray
for himself. When I become discouraged and wonder if he's going
to make it, I praise you that your heart is with us. When I grieve
over his mistakes and their consequences, you remind me of your
patience and forgiveness. When he's wounded or weak, your Word
tells me you're our healer. When I feel like we're in a daily battle with
one another, you declare that you're our peace. Thank you for your
wisdom when I'm foolish, your knowledge when I don't have a clue,
and your outpouring of mercy when I'm ready to quit.

Show me how to pray. Open my eyes to see what my son needs
most. I can fall into praying for an easy, happy life for him, but "what
does it profit a man to gain the whole world and forfeit his soul?"
(Mark 8:36 ESV). Guide my prayers so I can lift up his very soul to
you.

Make me faithful in prayer for my son. Teach me the mystery
of how to "Rejoice always, pray continually, give thanks in all circumstances; for this is God's will for you in Christ Jesus" (1 Thess.
5:16–18). I want to lift my son up to you at all times. I want to be
joyful and thankful even when he's troubled or rebellious. I want to
place him in your hands so I don't bear the weight of his future on
my own shoulders.

Thank you for the gift of prayer. You are always with me. You
never fail to listen and respond when I cry out to you. You care when
I'm hurting and afraid. You cover my mistakes as a parent with your
perfect love. And most of all, you love my son and know him through
and through. I praise your name for the hope we have in you—we are
saved and we are yours forever. Amen.

NOTES

1. Ann Voskamp, "Sons, Mothers, and Silk Purses out of Sow's Ears," *A Holy Experience*, April 7, 2011, http://www.aholyexperience.com/2011/04/sons-mothers-and-silk-purses-out-of-sows-ears/.

2. C. S. Lewis, *The Business of Heaven: Daily Readings from C. S. Lewis* (New York: Mariner Books, 1984), 22.

3. Christian Quotes, "Oswald Chambers," accessed September 26, 2013, http://christian-quotes.ochristian.com/Oswald-Chambers-Quotes/page-3.shtml.

4. Chuck Colson, "Finding Sexual Freedom in Augustine's Confessions," The Gospel Coalition, January 16, 2014, http://thegospelcoalition.org/blogs/tgc/2014/01/16/finding-sexual-freedom-in-augustines-confessions/.

5. Rob Jackson, "When Children View Pornography," Focus on the Family, accessed April 16, 2014, http://www.focusonthefamily.com/parenting/sexuality/when_children_use_pornography.aspx.

6. John Calvin, as quoted in Chris Tiegreen, *The One Year at His Feet Devotional* (Wheaton: Tyndale Momentum, 2006), 24.

7. D. L. Moody, *Mornings with Moody* (Dallas: Primedia eLaunch, 2012), 36.

8. Dr. Tim Kimmel, *Raising Kids Who Turn Out Right* (Scottsdale, AZ: Family Matters, 2006).

9. Dr. Chap Clark and Dr. Kara E. Powell, *Sticky Faith: Everyday Ideas to Build Lasting Faith in Your Kids* (Grand Rapids: Zondervan, 2011), 65.

Rob Teigen was a publishing professional for more than twenty years and is the author of the bestselling Laugh-Out-Loud Jokes for Kids series (under the pseudonym Rob Elliott). He and his wife, Joanna Teigen, have celebrated twenty-five years of marriage and have five kids who bring adventure to their lives in West Michigan. Together they create resources to encourage couples and families, including *88 Great Daddy-Daughter Dates*. Learn more at www.growinghome together.com.

Make Memories
with Your Daughter

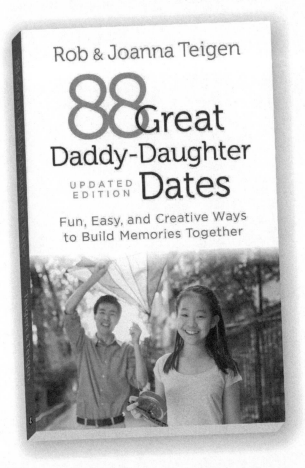

Make the most of your time with your daughter with these fun, easy, and creative dates! From bird-watching and making paper airplanes to bowling and photo scavenger hunts, there's something for every dad and his little girl.

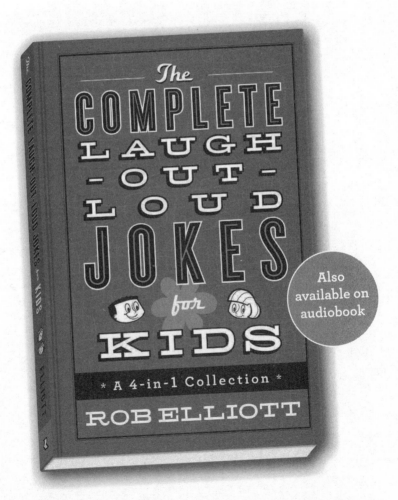

Little Books,
BIG LAUGHS